About IFPRI

The International Food Policy Research Institute (IFPRI®) was established in 1975 to identify and analyze alternative national and international strategies and policies for meeting food needs of the developing world on a sustainable basis, with particular emphasis on low-income countries and on the poorer groups in those countries. While the research effort is geared to the precise objective of contributing to the reduction of hunger and malnutrition, the factors involved are many and wide-ranging, requiring analysis of underlying processes and extending beyond a narrowly defined food sector. The Institute's research program reflects worldwide collaboration with governments and private and public institutions interested in increasing food production and improving the equity of its distribution. Research results are disseminated to policymakers, opinion formers, administrators, policy analysts, researchers, and others concerned with national and international food and agricultural policy.

About IFPRI Research Monographs

IFPRI Research Monographs are well-focused, policy-relevant monographs based on original and innovative research conducted at IFPRI. All manuscripts submitted for publication as IFPRI Research Monographs undergo extensive external and internal reviews. Prior to submission to the Publications Review Committee, each manuscript is circulated informally among the author's colleagues. Upon submission to the Committee, the manuscript is reviewed by an IFPRI reviewer and presented in a formal seminar. Three additional reviewers—at least two external to IFPRI and one from the Committee—are selected to review the manuscript. Reviewers are chosen for their familiarity with the country setting. The Committee provides the author its reaction to the reviewers' comments. After revising as necessary, the author resubmits the manuscript to the Committee with a written response to the reviewers' and Committee's comments. The Committee then makes its recommendations on publication of the manuscript to the Director General of IFPRI. With the Director General's approval, the manuscript becomes part of the IFPRI Research Monograph series. The publication series, under the original name of IFPRI Research Reports, began in 1977.

About IFPRI

The International Food Policy Research Institute (IFPRI) was established in 1975 to identify and analyze [illegible] and international strategies [illegible]

[illegible]

Human Capital Formation

History, Expectations, and Challenges in South Africa

Futoshi Yamauchi

RESEARCH MONOGRAPH

IFPRI®

INTERNATIONAL FOOD POLICY RESEARCH INSTITUTE

sustainable solutions for ending hunger and poverty

Supported by the CGIAR

International Food Policy Research Institute
2033 K Street, NW
Washington, D.C. 20006-1002, U.S.A.
Telephone +1-202-862-5600
www.ifpri.org

DOI: 10.2499/9780896291805

Library of Congress Cataloging-in-Publication Data

Yamauchi, Futoshi.
Human capital formation : history, expectations, and challenges in South Africa / Futoshi Yamauchi.
p. cm. – (IFPRI research monograph)
Includes bibliographical references and index.
ISBN 978-0-89629-180-5 (alk. paper)
1. Human capital—South Africa. 2. Economic development—Effect of education on—South Africa. 3. Economic development—Social aspects—South Africa. 4. Education—South Africa. I. Title. II. Series: IFPRI research monograph.
HD4904.7.Y343 2010
331.110968—dc22 2010038036

Contents

Tables

Figures

Acronyms and Abbreviations

ASSA	Actuarial Society of South Africa
EMIS	Education Management Information Systems
GIS	geographic information system
HOA	House of Assembly
HOD	House of Delegates
HOR	House of Representatives
IFPRI	International Food Policy Research Institute
KIDS	KwaZulu-Natal Income Dynamics Study
LER	learner-educator ratio
LFS	Labor Force Survey
OLS	ordinary least squares
PSLSD	Project for Statistics on Living Standards and Development
SGB	school governing body
SRN	School Register of Needs
TED	Transvaal Education Department

Summary

This research monograph is based on findings originally presented in Yamauchi (2005b) (Chapter 2), Yamauchi (2010) (Chapter 3), Yamauchi (2008) (Chapter 4), and Yamauchi, Buthelezi, and Velia (2008) (Chapter 5).

In Part 1, Chapter 2 presents evidence of changes in school quality in formerly white, colored, Indian/Asian, and African schools under the post-apartheid regime in South Africa. The analysis uses the learner-educator ratio as a measure of school quality. It is shown that although we observe some convergence in school quality, differences between formerly white and African schools are still significant. African schools are facing financial constraints in adjusting the number of teachers they can hire.

Chapter 3 demonstrates spatial patterns among heterogeneous schools and population groups. In particular, formerly white schools, which are shown to have better school quality, are located in communities where whites are dominant. Formerly white schools also charge higher school fees, which may screen out children from disadvantaged backgrounds. School fees are positively correlated with school quality in South Africa. Interestingly, empirical results show that dominant population groups in the community and former education departments are still significant determinants of school fees (quality), although in metropolitan areas local economic factors are also becoming important.

The second part of the chapter shows that both school fees and government subsidy increase the quality of education, decreasing the learner-educator ratio. In particular, an increase in government subsidy significantly increases the number of subsidized teachers. It is also found that government subsidy is allocated progressively to schools with initially poorer quality. The results imply that school fees can be decreased through an increase in government subsidy while maintaining school quality.

In Part 2, Chapter 4 analyzes dynamic human capital production from the early-childhood to schooling stages using panel data. Healthy growth in early childhood, measured by height-for-age *z*-scores, significantly improves schooling investments and outcomes, decreases the age at which school is started, decreases grade repetitions, and increases progression. However, for larger children, this effect is weak, possibly showing that health capital may increase the opportunity cost for schooling. Comparing the results from

6- and 11-year panel data, we can also conclude that the positive effect of early-childhood growth on schooling diminishes at higher schooling stages.

Chapter 5 addresses the effects of prime-age adult mortality on adolescents' transition from school to the labor market. First, we show that mortality is concentrated in prime-age adults. There are two types of responses to prime-age adult deaths: ex ante and ex post. Deaths of prime-age adults significantly increase both male and female adolescents' labor force participation as they stop their schooling. Second, the death of prime-age adults in general decreases school enrollment ex ante, but the effect is larger among male adolescents.

CHAPTER 1

Introduction

Human capital is a general notion of the knowledge and skills embodied in human beings, which plays an important role in determining their labor productivity (Schultz 1961; Becker 1962) and their ability to absorb new knowledge and master new technologies (Schultz 1975).

Human capital formation takes different forms and passes through various stages in parallel with the human life cycle. The core of human capital formation is acquisition of new knowledge and skills. There is no doubt in modern societies that education plays an important role in this central activity. However, since knowledge and skills are embodied in human beings, it is also hard to separate them from human health, which also determines labor productivity (for example, Strauss and Thomas 1995). Moreover, the interaction of human beings also affects knowledge spillovers in a society (Romer 1986; Lucas 1988). Therefore, the way in which the society is structured is crucial to the formation of human capital.

Formation starts before childbirth, when parents' decisions and behavior determine birth outcomes. Child growth affects outcomes during schooling (for example, Alderman et al. 2000), which subsequently influence labor market outcomes. It takes a long time to form human capital.

The fact that human capital is embodied in human beings implies that it can directly improve the earning capability of the poor. Human capital can contribute to greater equity in a society by directly changing the earning capability of those who have little access to physical and financial resources. Publicly funded education is one of the most important means of building human capital among the poor, who tend to be credit constrained for private investments in education. In this sense, human capital investment through public education is essentially open to the majority in many societies.

The accumulation of human capital is also a basis for economic growth. In many economies that have experienced successful economic growth, the accumulation of human capital either preceded the growth path, was an important component that explained growth, or both (Hayami and Godo 2005). Complementarities between human and physical capital in the economy lead to the acceleration of further investments in human and physical capital in the long run (Lucas 1988). The experiences in Asian economies show that human capital is one of many critical factors that can enhance economic growth with equity (World Bank 1993).

This monograph describes challenges and possibilities in the formation of human capital in South Africa. The country experienced apartheid until the mid-1990s. Given the difficulty in directly redistributing assets and wealth from the historically advantaged minority to the majority, the broad formation of human capital in the population—especially access to quality education among the majority Africans—appears to be able to provide more opportunities to the majority of Africans and to have the potential to improve equity in the country.[1]

Why Human Capital Is Important in South Africa

This monograph highlights the issues surrounding human capital formation in South Africa. Apartheid resulted in segregation and discrimination against the majority African population in almost all aspects of social life, such as education, employment, and residence. As part of apartheid, Africans were deprived of both physical and human assets, being forced to live on infertile land or in urban townships, and of the rights of citizenship and political participation, particularly the right to vote.[2]

Since 1994 the South African government has promised to implement policies to help the majority of Africans to gain lost opportunities. However, since the redistribution of assets from the minority whites to the majority Africans has been politically challenging, the country has also taken more gradual measures to improve equity, without adversely affecting its economic performance.

In the area of public education, the government of South Africa formally terminated school segregation laws, but realities for African learners did not improve greatly (see Chapters 2 and 3). The government introduced the South African School Act (Republic of South Africa 1996a, 1996b) and the Norms and Standards for School Funding (Republic of South Africa 1998) to provide guidance in implementing a nonsegregated education system. Under apartheid, segregated schools were governed by racially separate government agencies according to their classification both by population groups (white, colored,

---

[1] This process could create inequalities among Africans during the transition period, when more high-quality schools are introduced to the African population. However, given the current gap in the quality of schools available to the races, especially whites and Africans, the above-mentioned change is expected to narrow the gap in earnings in the labor market.

[2] Even before apartheid, Africans had been in an inferior situation for years. However, systematic legal structures that segregated and discriminated against Africans were enforced under apartheid.

Indian/Asian or African) and into independent and nonindependent homelands (see Chapter 2). In the post-apartheid regime, discriminatory and segregating barriers that prevented African children from entering other schools were discontinued. Yet in reality schools attended primarily by white children have maintained their superior quality over those attended by Africans. In spite of institutional reform, economic and spatial divides between whites and others have not changed significantly, and this reality is reflected in the education system. It is an urgent challenge to guarantee Africans access to quality education in the public system.[3]

Among the nations of the world, South Africa is ranked among the highest in terms of income inequality; its Gini coefficient is around 0.6. Given the difficulty in redistributing physical and financial assets, such as land, to Africans by drastic means, the formation of human capital in majority Africans appears to be one of the most feasible methods for improving equity in the society.[4] Regarding returns to education, the next section discusses features specific to the South African labor markets.

Human capital has several unique features. First, as already discussed, human capital directly improves individual earning capacity. Therefore, the formation of human capital among Africans would be expected to increase their earnings.

Second, through the public education system, the government is expected to progressively help the poor. Equal access to quality education plays a crucial role in guaranteeing this outcome.

Third, social returns are often larger than private returns. Externalities may arise from the accumulation of human capital in an economy, with human capital embodied in certain individuals augmenting that in others. This effect may also enhance the performance of the economy over the long run.

Fourth, and most importantly, the formation of human capital in a disadvantaged group builds new assets for that group. This strategy is entirely different from the redistribution of assets, in which certain assets are forcibly taken away from their owners. To secure equity in a society, a human-capital-based strategy is much less politically sensitive than one based on asset redistribution.[5] However, this strategy also has costs regarding the time that may be required for human capital investment to have an impact. It often

---

[3] This problem is different from that addressed by affirmative action, which seeks to guarantee equal opportunities to a minority group within a population.

[4] In the author's opinion, the inheritance tax should be systematically reformed so as to reduce nonlabor income components inheritable from the present generation to future generations. This channel will also increase the market supply of inheritable assets.

[5] A good example of the latter strategy is provided by Indonesia, where by presidential order oil surpluses in the 1970s were used to construct schools on a massive scale.

needs a rather long gestation period. For example, school education up to the completion of high school requires 12 years. This factor also implies that the expected improvement of equity and income distribution takes a rather long time.

Human capital investment needs time input, which implies opportunity cost at the individual level. Individuals need to indirectly pay the cost, forgoing earning opportunities that are available during the period they invest in human capital.

Returns to Education in South Africa

This section provides evidence on the returns to schooling in South African labor markets. Since I do not cover labor market issues in the main analysis, it is important to briefly discuss the functioning of labor markets and point out unique features of the markets in South Africa.

High unemployment is one key feature of the South African labor markets. Kingdon and Knight (2006) estimate that, in the period between 2002 and 2005, the unemployment rate was holding at 40 percent.

Several studies provide evidence on returns to schooling in the South African labor markets using micro data (see Bhorat et al. 2001). Though racial gaps in returns to schooling have been narrowed, lower returns among Africans are attributed to grade repetition and the lower quality of the schools available to them (for example, Anderson, Case, and Lam 2001).

One interesting aspect of the data on schooling returns is their convexity. Education up to the high school level does not contribute to employment, but tertiary-level education significantly increases the probability of employment (Bhorat et al. 2001), thus creating convexity in the earning profile. This finding is similar to reports from the Philippines (Yamauchi 2005a).

The effect of heterogeneity in school quality on labor market outcomes is important in South Africa. For example, Case and Yogo (1999) attempted to quantify the effect of school quality on labor market earnings in South Africa, merging data from population censuses and school censuses.[6] On this point, it is worth noting that the matriculation pass rate at high school graduation is generally low in South Africa, having decreased from 70 percent in 2004 to 65 percent in 2007. This means that even if children officially finish high school, they are not qualified based on measures of educational accomplishment. The problem is particularly severe in rural areas where schools are located in predominantly African communities.

[6] Case and Deaton (1999) examined the effect of school quality on learner performance.

The September 2003 Labor Force Survey (LFS) reveals some basic features of the South African labor markets, with special attention to returns to schooling. Figures 1.1 and 1.2 show the distributions of years of schooling completed for age groups 15-39 and 40-64 in the LFS sample.

These graphs demonstrate the convergence of educational attainment across population groups over cohorts. The distribution among whites has been constant between the age groups. Note the large increase in schooling attainment among younger cohorts in the Indian/Asian group, enabling the distribution for that group to be nearly equivalent to that of whites. Though increases in completed schooling are observed in the African and colored groups, the average level is far below the levels of whites and Indian/Asians.

Figure 1.1 Years of schooling completed: Ages 15-39

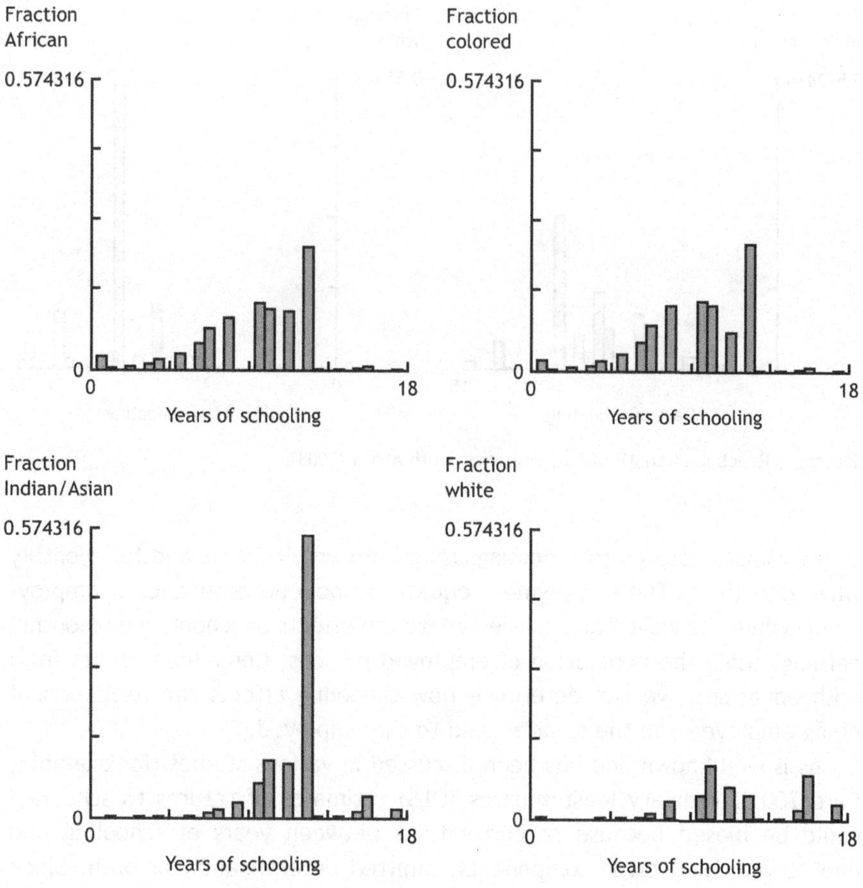

Source: Republic of South Africa, Statistics South Africa (2003).

Figure 1.2 Years of schooling completed: Ages 40-64

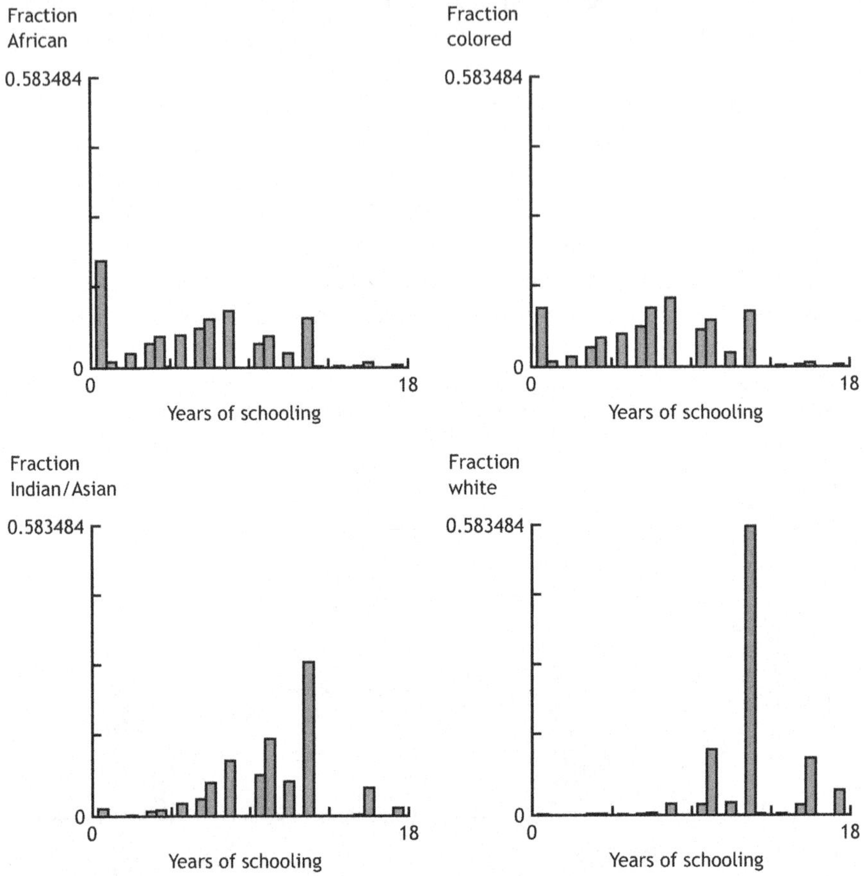

Source: Republic of South Africa, Statistics South Africa (2003).

I estimate returns to schooling using both employment and log monthly wage equations. The employment equations show determinants of employment, while the wage equations estimate the effects of schooling on monthly earnings using the population of employed persons. Combining results from both equations, we can determine how schooling affects the likelihood of being employed and the salaries paid to the employed.

As is well known and has been discussed in various studies (for example, Card 2001), ordinary least squares (OLS) estimates of returns to schooling could be biased because of correlations between years of schooling and unobserved fixed error components, omitted determinants, or both. Since individual ability (augmenting the wage) and schooling attainment are positively correlated, our estimates are likely to be biased upward.[7]

Moreover, school quality and family background (neither of which is directly observable) affect schooling attainment and income levels. In the current context, they are both correlated with population groups: whites still have persistently better access to high-quality schools and enjoy more family resources than the other groups, particularly Africans. Therefore it is important to control for population groups to minimize potential bias in estimating returns to schooling.

Columns 1–3 in Table 1.1 summarize estimation results for the employment equation.[8] Schooling significantly increases the probability of having work (column 1), but it only increases the probability if high school or a higher level is attained (column 2). Educational attainment up to grade 12 does not significantly contribute to the likelihood of being employed in South Africa.

Column 3 includes the interaction of population group indicators and years of schooling. Whites have an advantage in getting employment, and Indian/Asians have a disadvantage regardless of schooling, compared to Africans. However, returns to schooling are significantly higher among coloreds and Indian/Asians than Africans.

Chapter 5 presents empirical evidence on transitions among adolescents from school to the labor market, highlighting the impacts of prime-age adult mortality. Many adolescents who quit school do not find jobs in the labor market (increasing the labor supply in the labor force).

Similar findings are confirmed by the wage equations (columns 4–6). One interesting finding is that, compared to Africans, whites earn higher wages regardless of schooling, and Indian/Asians demonstrate higher returns to schooling. It is also confirmed that schooling up to completion of high school does not contribute to monthly wage.

These findings demonstrated heterogeneity in returns to schooling in both the employment and wage equations, but they also pose two as yet unresolved

---

[7] In the empirical setting and for the data used in the estimation of returns to schooling, it is difficult to find valid instruments or exogenous variations in years of schooling (schooling attainment). Schooling attainment increased in the recent cohorts, especially among Africans after 1994, but in the post-apartheid regime the change occurred simultaneously with changes in the labor markets, such as employment opportunities formerly restricted to whites being opened to Africans.

[8] The employment indicator takes the value of one if an individual works in some capacity and zero otherwise. I dropped from the sample those who did not look for work within the past seven days because they are currently learners, housewives (homemakers), retired (prefer not to seek work), ill, disabled, too young, or too old. The indicator takes a value of one if the individual is guaranteed work in the near future.

Second, we analyze household behavior related to human capital investment. In this area, we focus on dynamic human capital production, from early-childhood nutrition intake to schooling investments and attainment, and on adolescents' transition to the labor market. Even at this stage of the analysis, it is important to integrate institutional factors and observed household behavior to achieve a comprehensive understanding.

In South Africa, access to quality education is still highly unequal across population groups and locations, although the situation has been changing. In the transition from apartheid to a democratic education system, two milestones stand out: the 1996 South African School Act and the 1998 Norms and Standards for School Funding. These two sets of rules provided basic guidelines to departments of education at the national and provincial levels. More recently, South Africa introduced a revised set of Norms and Standards to promote more progressive fiscal interventions in the school system.

As described in Part 1, however, there still remain discrepancies in access to quality education across population groups and communities (where population groups remain locally clustered). To understand institutional constraints, the two key dimensions are introduced.

The first dimension is population groups. Historically there have been four politically defined population groups in the country: white, colored, Indian/Asian, and African. The majority of the population is African. Under apartheid, Africans had semiautonomous homelands where they governed and received almost no support from the white central government. Public schools were also governed by different education ministries that were separated by population group and homeland. It has been important to investigate the convergence in access to quality education across population groups.

The second dimension is location. Since population groups were segregated in residential locations under apartheid, their schools were also segregated by location. For example, African schools were located in predominantly African communities. Therefore access to quality education has a spatial dimension. Since commuting long distances to school is not possible for many children owing to the substantial financial and time costs involved, accessibility to good schools depends on their spatial distribution (and on changes to that distribution, given past conditions).

In Part 2 findings on household behavior using micro panel data are reported. In particular, this part examines the dynamic nature of human capital investments and formation, from early-childhood growth (nutrition intake), to schooling investments, to adolescents' transition to the labor market. Chapter 4 focuses on dynamic human capital production in which early-stage investment can have long-term implications for schooling outcomes (and therefore potentially labor market outcomes).

In the analysis of school-to-market transition, it is important to note that South Africa has suffered from unusually high levels of unemployment (or underemployment), which makes the transition from school to labor markets quite difficult (see also results in Table 1.1). Individuals, while in the labor force, do not necessarily transition to employment. In Chapter 5 I identify the impacts of prime-adult mortality, prevalent in recent years because of HIV/AIDS, on adolescent labor supply behavior under circumstances in which completion of high school or higher-level schooling significantly increases the likelihood of being employed.

This shock might have affected human capital formation by reducing parental inputs to child schooling and increasing the need for school-age individuals to look for work. Perceived returns to human capital investment (for example, schooling) may also be altered owing to an increase in prime-age adult mortality.

Data Sources

School and Population Census

The analysis in Part 1 uses three datasets: (1) School Register of Needs (SRN) 1996 and 2000, (2) Annual School Surveys (School Census), (3) Census 2001 Community Profile (with geographic information system [GIS] data), and (4) KwaZulu-Natal Department of Education School Finance data. The SRN and Annual School Surveys comprise census data on schools. The former has quite detailed information on school facilities, while the latter is more general, containing information on learners and school finance.

In the analysis of the spatial distribution of school quality and population groups (Chapter 3), I also use the Community Profile Database in the 2001 population census. Since GIS information is available in both school censuses, it was possible to merge the population census and school census data by location. In addition, I use government subsidy data provided by the KwaZulu-Natal Department of Education to analyze the effect of such subsidies on school quality. Details on school data are supplied in Chapters 2 and 3.

KwaZulu-Natal Income Dynamics, Rounds 2 and 3

In the analysis of household behavior, I rely on the KwaZulu-Natal Income Dynamics Study (KIDS), rounds 2 and 3, conducted in 1998 and 2004, respectively.[9] The data were collected in the province of KwaZulu-Natal in 1993

---

[9] The KwaZulu-Natal Income Dynamics Study was a collaborative project between researchers at the International Food Policy Research Institute (IFPRI), the University of KwaZulu-Natal, the University of Wisconsin, the London School of Hygiene and Tropical Medicine, the Norwegian

during surveys for the Project for Statistics on Living Standards and Development (PSLSD) by the South African Labour and Development Research Unit. Though spatial coverage is restricted to the province, these are unique panel data that started before the transition from apartheid to democracy.[10]

KIDS involved three rounds: round 1 in 1993, round 2 in 1998, and round 3 in 2004. Compilation of the dataset, which is focused on the gathering of income and expenditure data via a detailed questionnaire, followed the national PSLSD, which was carried out across South Africa in 1993 and managed by the World Bank. As such, KIDS round 1 is a geographic *subset* of households from the national survey, with colored and white households excluded from follow-up.

The sampling frame for the 1993 national survey was based on a two-stage self-weighting design. The 1991 Census Enumerator Subdistrict (or an equivalent unit such as a village or village group) was the first-stage unit; systematic sampling was then applied to households within that unit during the second sampling stage (see South African Labour and Development Research Unit 1994 for further details).

In 2004 data were collected for 1,426 African and Indian/Asian households across 68 (rural and urban) "clusters" in KwaZulu-Natal; 867 households interviewed contained key decisionmakers in 1993 (see May et al. 2007 for further details on the survey). In round 3 information was collected on about 65 percent of the 1998 household members.[11]

The 2004 survey in particular collected some retrospective information on child schooling, such as repetitions and school-start age. Combining these data with anthropometry measures for 1993 and 1998, I can analyze dynamic

---

Institute of Urban and Regional Studies, and the South African Department of Social Development. In addition to support from these institutions, the following organizations provided financial support: the Department for International Development South Africa (DFID-SA), the United States Agency for International Development (USAID), the Andrew W. Mellon Foundation, and the National Research Foundation Norwegian Research Council, through a grant to the University of KwaZulu-Natal.

[10] More recent panel data from the country include: four rounds of the Cape Area Panel Study, a longitudinal study of the lives of youths and young adults in metropolitan Cape Town (see www.caps.uct.ac.za for details), two demographic surveillance sites providing annually collected panel data on 11,000 households in Limpopo province since the early 1990s (Agincourt Health and Population Unit), and twice-yearly panel data on 11,000 households in KwaZulu-Natal since 2000 (Africa Centre for Health and Population Studies).

[11] May et al. (2007) describe the methodology of the KIDS survey and its history. They show that the follow-up rate was comparatively high for women (relative to men) and for those less than 20 years old in 1998, as these subgroups are comparatively less mobile than other groups. They note that there may have been problems of representativity from round 1. Nevertheless they show that the age distribution, sex ratio, and change by age in the sex ratio of household members (including the children of core household members who were tracked at times outside KwaZulu-Natal) in 2004 are generally representative of the trends for the province when set against the 2001 census data. Children 10–14 years old are overrepresented in KIDS, while younger adults are underrepresented; the authors provide detailed explanation for these situations.

human capital formation from early-childhood to school stages (Chapter 4). In the analysis in Chapter 4, I also use some information from the 1993 survey.

In the analysis of adolescent transition from school to the labor market (Chapter 5), I use prime-age adult deaths as external shocks to adolescents who change the timing of their entrance into the labor force. In the period from 1998 to 2004, South Africa (and KwaZulu-Natal in particular) experienced a high prime-age mortality rate. In the face of increased prime-age adult mortality, human behavior has been changed to mitigate its adverse impacts.[12]

[12] In Chapter 5, I discuss some important differences between our results and other studies in the literature.

PART 1

Institutions

Part 1 describes the school system in post-apartheid South Africa. The focus is on quality gaps across schools, which have been persistent since the time of apartheid. Chapter 2 analyzes differences in school quality, measured by the learner-educator ratio, across former white, colored, Indian/Asian, and African schools, using school census data. Chapter 3 examines school fees, which are also indicative of school quality in a system in which schools and communities must raise needed resources; the findings demonstrate that school quality is spatially correlated with residential patterns of different population groups. It is also shown that government subsidy can improve school quality and lower school fees. From both analyses, we conclude that financial constraints seem still to be binding at both the school and community levels in South Africa.

CHAPTER 2

Race, Equity, and Public Schools in the First Decade of Post-Apartheid South Africa

In the transition from apartheid to a democratic society in South Africa after the first democratic national election in 1994, the government promised to provide equal opportunities for education to all racial groups and regions (Republic of South Africa 1996a, 1996b). However, as reported in *Education Atlas of South Africa* (Bot, Wilson, and Dove 2000), there still exist wide variations in major indicators of educational quality across regions. Given the clustered spatial distribution of racial groups in the country, it is not difficult to infer variations in educational opportunities among children across different population groups. In this chapter, I use South African school census data from 1996 and 2000 to assess variations in educational quality of public schools across former population groups and investigate changes in post-apartheid South Africa.

It has been recognized both inside and outside South Africa that under apartheid (over which the African population had no control) African schools—for example, those in the former homelands—were totally inferior to white schools in terms of funding (Kriege et al. 1994; Marais 1995; Crouch 1996). Differences in conditions between African and non-African schools led to corresponding differences in learner achievement, particularly examination scores in numeracy (Case and Deaton 1999). Unless the government actively strengthens its support of former African schools in terms of budget and personnel allocations, in order to narrow apartheid-created differences in educational quality, a vicious cycle of poverty and low-quality education will persist. Children who cannot receive a sufficiently high quality of education are less likely to be engaged in regular employment and are therefore more likely to remain in the low-income class (for example, Case and Yogo 1999). Since they cannot afford to live in well-off residential areas (in many cases, former white areas), which typically have high-quality schools, they are likely to stay in areas with inferior schools. When high residential rents prohibit access to better schools, this cycle will persist, potentially becoming a crucial determinant of the long-term poverty trap for Africans in the country.

To study gaps in educational quality across population groups, I focus on the ratio of learners to educators (teachers and other staff)—the learner-educator ratio (LER)—from two school censuses, SRN 1996 and 2000. In 1995 the government reached an agreement that ratios of 40:1 and 35:1 were to be achieved for primary and secondary schools, respectively, in the next five years. Therefore, LER can provide a good indicator not only of the distribution of education quality but also of the government's policy interventions to achieve educational equity.

Recent empirical work shows significant effects of LER and class size on learner achievement, although the literature as a whole contains some ambiguity (Hanushek 1998). The difficulty in identifying causality arises from potential endogeneity in the number of learners and unobserved fixed components specific to school and community, which is likely to be correlated with school inputs.[1] For example, Lazear (2001) argues that the effect of LER on learner achievement could be empirically ambiguous because of (often unobserved) heterogeneity in learner quality, that is, discipline. In his model, the optimal size of a class (LER) increases if learner discipline improves, since the probability of disruption in a classroom decreases. To avoid such a correlation between LER and unobservables, recent studies use exogenous variations (changes) in LER and class size to identify the effect on learner achievement (for example, Angrist and Lavy 1999; Case and Deaton 1999; Krueger 1999; Hoxby 2000). In these studies with exogenous variations in LER, the effect is found to be significant. In the context of South Africa, Case and Deaton (1999) show that among Africans under apartheid who were not free to choose schools, LER has a significant effect on learner achievement, particularly in numeracy, while its effect is not significant among whites.

Table 2.1 compares means of LERs by population groups in both 1996 and 2000. A striking fact evident from the table is that the gap between formerly African and white schools did not narrow during the period. Formerly white schools maintained their superior situation in the post-apartheid period. Though more detailed statistical analysis is provided in the section on empirical findings, the difference between formerly African and white schools seems persistent and stable.

The LER gaps can have long-term implications. For instance, school quality matters in subsequent labor market outcomes (Card and Krueger 1996; Case and Yogo 1999; Dustman, Rajah, and Soest 2003). Based on Case and

---

[1] High LERs are partly attributed to high grade repetition rates in South Africa. However, those who have repeated grades are more likely to transition to labor markets (Yamauchi 2003, using data from the KwaZulu-Natal Income Dynamics Study).

Table 2.1 Learner-educator ratios by population group, 1996 and 2000

Population group	African	White	Colored	Indian/Asian	New schools
Primary school					
1996	36.211	26.151	28.736	27.753	39.673
2000	31.465	25.790	29.996	32.806	40.833
Secondary school					
1996	31.975	22.329	23.196	23.415	38.145
2000	31.052	24.203	30.157	30.447	35.996

Sources: Republic of South Africa, Department of Education (1996, 2000).
Note: Sample means are shown by population group.

Yogo's estimates of the impact of LER on returns to schooling investments, for example, the marginal effect of LER on rate of return is around 0.002. The mean LER gap between formerly African and white primary schools, 10.060 in 1996 (Table 2.1), is equivalent to a reduction of 0.0201 in the rate of returns. The reduction is substantial because the average rate of return was 0.089–0.094 for men age 24–28 in 1996. Thus we can infer that inequality in educational opportunities (that is, gaps in LER) is transformed into inequality in labor market earning opportunities in South Africa.[2]

The organization of this chapter is as follows. The next section sets up a simple framework in which liquidity constraint is highlighted. The following section describes the data that I use in the analysis, SRN 1996 and 2000. The surveys focus particularly on school facility information, in addition to basic information such as the numbers of educators and learners.[3] To identify the former racial groups of those schools, SRN 2000 provides information on the departments that governed the schools under apartheid. Therefore, merging the two surveys, I can systematically track former apartheid departments. I exclude from the analysis of the sample the provinces of Gauteng, Mpumalanga, and Northern Cape since they changed school registration codes

[2] Yamauchi (2003) shows that grade repetition increases the probability of transition from school to labor market in South Africa and that it adversely affects employment probability, particularly for men. Other conditions being equal, grade repetition is positively correlated with LER, as more learners remain enrolled longer.

[3] However, the SRN lacks information on financial conditions and learner performance. In recent years, the Annual School Surveys have started collecting information on school facilities. In previous studies using SRN 1996, Bot, Wilson, and Dove (2000) completed a districtwise characterization of school environments from various perspectives. The National Department of Education (2002) conducted a provincial-level characterization of SRN 1996 and 2000 and described dynamic changes in South African education. In these studies, however, the data were not analyzed statistically.

(Education Management Information Systems [EMIS] codes) after 1996, preventing an accurate merge of the 1994 and 2000 datasets.[4]

In the section on empirical findings we see, first, that the LER distribution for formerly African schools differs from that of formerly white, colored, Indian/Asian, and new schools in both 1996 and 2000. In particular, the difference between formerly African schools and white or Indian/Asian schools was found to be statistically significant. A large number of formerly African schools exhibit LERs above the targets set by the government: 40:1 and 35:1 for primary and secondary schools, respectively.

To identify how the number of educators was adjusted in response to changes in the number of learners, the estimation strategy takes into account community-school-level unobserved fixed components, using specifications drawn directly from the model in the appendix. First, the adjustments of educators in responding to changes in the number of learners (with budget constraints) differ statistically across racial groups in primary schools, especially the adjustments of subsidized educators. Formerly African schools are more budget (liquidity) constrained than non-African (white, colored, and Indian/Asian) schools when they employ educators. Second, among secondary schools, the gaps are smaller than those found in primary schools. Interestingly, formerly white secondary schools do not show any significant adjustments to changes in the number of learners during this period, probably because their condition was already optimal. Third, in combined schools (both primary and secondary levels), the gaps between formerly African and Indian/Asian or new schools are significant. This observation reflects the fact that combined schools are regionally concentrated in certain districts and that there are few formerly white schools of this type. Fourth, in the analysis restricted to nonsubsidized (privately employed) educators, the number of educators does not significantly respond to changes in the number of learners. In this sense, the liquidity constraint is more binding at the school level than at the government level.

Framework

Setting

I factor out possible reasons for changes in the number of learners. First, natural population growth contributes to cohort size, and therefore the number of school-age children in a community. Second, after the abolition of apartheid, households could freely migrate from formerly African areas to

[4] Since its population size is large, exclusion of Gauteng may potentially affect our results.

white areas. Third, parents can send their children to live with distant family members or foster in other children, or children can go to private schools that formerly belonged to different population groups, even though these schools are not located in their residential areas.[5]

In response to cross-sectional differences as well as changes in the number of learners in public schools, it is desirable to adjust the number of educators optimally to maintain efficiency in learning and equity among children. There are several scenarios. Consider a stationary environment in which the total number of learners does not change. If the provincial government coordinates the employment of teachers and allocates them among schools with no transaction costs, the optimal ratio of learners to educators can be smoothly maintained. The ratios will be equalized across schools.

If schools have discretion over the employment of educators independently of the local government (for example, principals decide to employ teachers with the approval of school governing bodies consisting of community leaders, parents, and educators), the adjustment of educators depends on decisionmaking in each school and mostly on its financial condition. Currently in South Africa, many public schools receive insufficient financial support from the government. In this case, equalization of the ratios is not guaranteed. In other words, the equalization of LERs is a necessary condition for, among other things, unitary decisionmaking (or interventions) by the government. Even if the local government suffers budget constraints, unitary decisionmaking will lead to the equalization of LERs.

In response to changes in the number of learners, budget constraints may matter at the school and government levels. Without population growth, under unitary decisionmaking by the government it is easy to transfer educators from one school to another to equalize ratios across schools. This is especially important under the post-apartheid regime, in which people are essentially free to migrate. With population growth, however, to maintain the current LER, the adjustment of educators (like the adjustment of capital stock) depends on the government's budget (liquidity) constraint, since the government needs new educators.

When public schools receive little or no government subsidy, the situation is more serious. Schools with binding budget constraints that cannot collect enough school fees from learner households are likely to have great difficulty in hiring more educators. Unlike with unitary decisionmaking, there will be more variations in LER across schools in this case, since financial conditions

[5] Zimmerman (2003) shows that fostering raises school enrollment in South Africa. The geographic movement of children is partly motivated by the attempt to provide them with better educational opportunities.

are likely to be different between schools. As a result, for quasi-privatized and budget-constrained public schools, LERs could have wide variations in cross-section as well as time series. The appendix presents a simple model that formalizes this idea.

Empirical Specification, Identification, and Estimation

In the empirical analysis, I estimate a response function of educators to learners taking into account school budget condition:

$$H_{it} = [I(y^* > \phi_{it})\beta^* + I(y^* < \phi_{it})\gamma_{it}(p)]L_{it} + \mu_i + \varepsilon_{it}, \tag{2.1}$$

where $\beta^* \geq \gamma_{it}(p)$, p denotes population group, and μ_i is the fixed effect that reflects unobserved school- and community-specific components. $I(y^* > \phi_{it})$ means that the school is not budget constrained, while $I(y^* < \phi_{it})$ means that it is budget constrained. In the latter case, adjustment of educators is lower than the optimal. The derivation of $\gamma_{it}(p)$ is given in the appendix. Here local condition f is also represented by population group p. Since, in the analysis using the SRN, the information on subsidies and school fees is not available, I assume the patterns according to which these two variables are determined differ across population groups. I estimate $\gamma_{it}(p)$ as a reduced-form parameter in the estimation of (2.1).

In equation (2.1), as in many cross-sectional studies, it is likely that the number of learners is correlated with the unobserved fixed component μ_i, which will bias the OLS estimate of the slope. For example, in communities experiencing rapid urbanization, where teachers can easily commute from urban centers and learners can migrate to them, the numbers of learners and educators will increase simultaneously. In this case, OLS estimates are biased upwardly. Assuming that parameters do not change over the four years, after conditioning on cross-group differences, we difference them between two periods:

$$\Delta H_{i \in p} = \sum_p \gamma_i(p) \Delta L_{i \in p} + \Delta\varepsilon_i, \tag{2.2}$$

where Δ is the differencing operator. The shocks are assumed to be ex post in each period.

The parameter of interest represents the degree of liquidity constraint. As we will see in the section "Distribution Comparison," the empirical distributions of LER motivate the analysis of determinants for the observed LER gaps across population groups. However, naive comparisons of LER distributions cannot identify school and government behavior—that is, how the number of educators changes in response to changes in the number of learners—and how likely liquidity constraint is to be binding in adjusting the number of educators. Changes in the number of learners represent fundamental changes in schools or the government that lead to adjustment in the number of educators.[6]

Since the main interest of this chapter is differences in school behavior across population groups, we group schools into five groups—African, white, colored, Indian/Asian, and others (new schools)—in equation (2.2). I use race-group dummies to approximate differences in patterns where liquidity and subsidy constraints bind decisionmaking regarding the employment of educators. In this framework, we cannot distinguish whether the liquidity-cum-resource constraint is binding or the target ratio is different across the groups. I exclude the latter case here. In the estimation, I also use magisterial district dummies so that we capture variations across population groups within districts, in which schools and communities are more homogeneous than those in an entire province. By focusing on within-district cross-race differences, we can identify how differentially the liquidity constraint is binding the decision on adjusting the number of educators across population groups. In the null hypothesis that the entire budget is pooled over all population groups, the liquidity (budget) constraint should bind equally for all the groups.

The estimation of equation (2.2) requires additional consideration. It is possible for the past shock in the number of educators (ε_{i1}) to partly cause subsequent changes in the number of learners, $E[\Delta L_{i\in p}\varepsilon_{i1}] \neq 0$. Suppose that a positive shock to the number of educators increases the incentives for potential learners to attend the school. This positive correlation leads to a negative bias in the OLS estimator in equation (2.2). In this sense, the endogenous movement (decisionmaking) of learners influences the magnitude of the negative bias. Under this circumstance, it is likely that the true value of the slope is somewhere between a possibly upwardly biased estimate from the cross-sectional analysis in equation (2.1) and a possibly downwardly biased estimate from the panel analysis in equation (2.2).[7]

---

[6] The approach we are taking looks similar to the one used in studies of liquidity constraint in firms' investment behavior. However, in this method investment is regressed on changes in sales revenue that represent exogenous shocks. The null hypothesis is that changes in sales revenue have no effect on investment without liquidity constraint.

[7] In Yamauchi (2005b) I used the instrumental variable approach to control for the endogeneity of changes in the number of learners. The first-stage estimation results are interesting since they show how the government can predict ex ante the number of future learners.

Data Sources

SRN, with its main focus on the conditions of school facilities, was initially fielded in 1996. In that survey, trained fieldworkers attempted to visit all schools in the country and collected information from educators, mainly school principals. Although the survey's coverage was found to be imperfect because some schools were not accessible during the survey preparation stage, this was the first systematic school census in the country. Schools were identified by school codes provided by provincial departments of education (EMIS codes) and by province codes, and also by latitude and longitude using a global positioning system.

Four years later, the National Department of Education conducted the second round of the survey. This time, however, data were collected through questionnaires distributed to school principals. This means of data collection alerts us to possible errors in the recorded answers, especially those concerning facility conditions: principals might want to attempt to get more funding by underreporting their school facilities, for example, building condition and the number of classrooms. To minimize this problem, the questionnaire was designed to elicit only changes from 1996 conditions, which were described on the distributed form.

Yet even with potential measurement errors and bias in some questions, the 2000 survey accomplished almost-perfect coverage of schools in the country. In particular, fieldworkers visited those schools that were missed in SRN 1996. Unlike SRN 1996, the 2000 version does not include technical colleges and special schools, but it completely covers all primary, secondary, and combined schools. (For detailed discussions of SRN 1996 and 2000, see EduAction 2001.) The data that I use here were provided by EduAction, Durban, and the National Department of Education, Pretoria. Table 2.2 shows summary statistics.

For the purpose of constructing panel data, it is important to note that EMIS codes are also available in SRN 2000. However, some provincial departments of education changed their EMIS codes after 1996, and the details of the code changes are not transparent. Therefore I decided to include only provinces that used the same EMIS codes in 2000 as in 1996. As a result, Gauteng, Mpumalanga and Northern Cape are excluded from our sample for the analysis that follows.

Another important feature of SRN 2000 for our purposes is that it asked about former departments that governed the schools under the apartheid regime. From this information, we can correctly identify the racial background of each school under the previous regime. The correspondence between former departments and population groups is as follows:

- Whites—Department of Education and Culture: House of Assembly
- Whites—Transvaal Education Department

Table 2.2 Summary statistics

Variable	Number of observations	Mean	Standard deviation	Minimum	Maximum
Public primary schools					
Learners 1996	6,214	400.0599	366.1124	3	5,292
Educators 1996	6,234	11.62624	10.11832	1	68
Learner-educator ratio 1996	6,168	34.02758	16.88301	1	536
Learners 2000	9,170	305.1333	307.7398	1	3,711
Educators 2000	9,422	9.066546	11.68714	1	805
Learner-educator ratio 2000	9,170	31.55526	16.26099	0.0625	729
Public secondary schools					
Learners 1996	2,049	660.4461	399.2136	8	2,945
Educators 1996	2,046	23.33382	14.78122	1	90
Learner-educator ratio 1996	2,035	30.48634	12.53213	1	150
Learners 2000	4,316	578.0461	350.3784	1	2,648
Educators 2000	4,455	19.08485	11.46771	1	94
Learner-educator ratio 2000	4,316	31.18687	10.08921	0.3333	179
Public primary schools					
Change in number of learners	5,366	-24.07697	161.6493	-3,986	2,692
Change in number of educators	5,572	-0.6281407	4.100372	-49	104
Public secondary schools					
Change in number of learners	1,830	-21.81639	231.2277	-2,225	1,014
Change in number of educators	1,913	-1.934135	7.070909	-46	67

Sources: Republic of South Africa, Department of Education (1996, 2000).

Notes: Primary schools in 1996 include normal primary (grades 1-7), junior primary (grades 1-4), and senior primary schools (grades 5-8). Secondary schools in 1996 include normal secondary (grades 8-12), junior secondary (grades 8-10), and senior secondary schools (grades 10-12). Primary schools in 2000 refer to those with lowest grade 1 or higher and highest grade 7 or lower. Secondary schools in 2000 refer to those with lowest grade 8 or higher and highest grade 12 or lower. Public schools in 1996 include state and state-aided schools. Sample excludes Gauteng, Mpumalanga, and Northern Cape provinces.

- Colored—Department of Education and Culture: House of Representatives
- Indian/Asian—Department of Education and Culture: House of Delegates
- African—Bophuthatswana Education Department
- African—Ciskei Education Department
- African—Department of Education and Training
- African—Gazankulu Department of Education
- African—KaNgwane Department of Education
- African—KwaNdebele Department of Education
- African—KwaZulu Department of Education and Culture
- African—Lebowa Department of Education
- African—QwaQwa Department of Education
- African—Transkei Education Department

- African—Venda Education Department
- All races—New schools established after 1994, New Education Department

Under the post-apartheid regime, children of any racial origin can attend any school. In our analysis, those schools established after the end of apartheid are grouped as "new schools." It should be emphasized here that, even though schools are sorted by former departments, the period covered by our analysis falls after apartheid. Therefore, all schools are theoretically race-free in both 1996 and 2000. However, the reality of the racial composition of learners did not change substantially until 2000. The majority of formerly African schools are still in communities that are predominantly African, so the learners in those schools are still mostly African. Some formerly white schools now accept children from African families that have relatively high incomes and reside within commuting distance. Therefore—although my focus on population groups is approximate, as it does not reflect the exact racial composition of each school—I can capture the essence of social distance across racial groups in South Africa, where most schools and communities are still racially homogeneous even after apartheid.[8]

Empirical Findings

Three types of empirical analyses are conducted here. First, I statistically characterize the distributions of LERs in 1996 and 2000 in different population groups. Cumulative distributions of LER are compared and Kolmogorov-Smirnov tests are used for statistical comparisons of LER distributions of formerly African schools with other schools. Second, I depict the relationship between changes in educators and learners for each population group. Third, I conduct a panel analysis that differences out fixed effects to estimate the response of the number of learners to the number of educators.

Distribution Comparison

Figures 2.1 and 2.2 show LER distributions in public primary and secondary schools for 1996 and 2000, respectively. Primary (grades 1-7), junior primary

[8] However, the information on former departments is available only in SRN 2000, not in SRN 1996. It is therefore necessary to merge SRNs 1996 and 2000 by EMIS and provincial codes in order to group schools covered in SRN 1996 by population group. As a result of this merging process, excluding Gauteng, Mpumalanga, and Northern Cape for the reason mentioned earlier, nearly 10 percent of primary and secondary schools in SRN 1996 do not match those in SRN 2000. In the panel analysis of dynamic changes from 1996 to 2000 and in the cross-sectional analysis of differences across population groups in SRN 1996, I use only those schools that were correctly matched between SRN 1996 and SRN 2000.

(grades 1-4), and senior primary (grades 5-7) are aggregated as primary schools, and secondary (grades 8-12), junior secondary (grades 8-10), and senior secondary (grade 11-12) are grouped as secondary schools. In these figures, distributions are shown for schools for different former population groups—African (African), white, colored, Indian/Asian—and for new schools.

For formerly African and new schools, LER distributions have long upper tails. For the sake of display, values of LER larger than 200 were omitted in these graphs, though there are substantial numbers of formerly African and new schools in this range. On the other hand, the distributions are shown to be concentrated within a range of relatively small values for formerly white, colored, and Indian/Asian schools. This basic characterization of differences in LER distributions across former population groups is valid for all types of schools—primary and secondary. The main findings on cross-group differences are quite similar in both primary and secondary schools.

To statistically characterize differences in the LER distribution between formerly African schools and the other schools, I use Kolmogorov-Smirnov tests (Tables 2.3A and 2.3B). Table 2.3A shows two basic findings. First, in the country as a whole, the LER distributions of African primary and secondary schools are statistically different from those of white, colored, and Indian/Asian schools in 1996 and 2000. In particular, the test statistics show that the distance between African and white has not narrowed from 1996 to 2000.

Table 2.3B shows provincial-level results for the Kolmogorov-Smirnov tests. At the provincial level I find that the results differ between provinces in 1996 and 2000. In 1996 the distance between African and white primary schools is found to be significant in many provinces, except Free State and North West, where the distances to colored, Indian/Asian, and other groups are also insignificant. In 2000, however, African and white primary schools are significantly different in all provinces. In this case, the difference remains quite robust between African and white in post-apartheid South Africa. Findings for secondary schools are stronger than those for primary schools. In Free State and North West, where African and white are not different in primary schools, the distance is statistically significant in both 1996 and 2000.

The findings clearly confirm our prior perception that formerly African schools, at both the primary and secondary levels, have not improved relative to formerly white schools, even under the post-apartheid government. This finding does not directly imply that African children in the country suffer more severely from low quality of education than white children. In post-apartheid South Africa, all schools must not discriminate among children based on their origins, and children of any racial origin are selectively admitted. However, since most communities are still racially homogeneous, the

Figure 2.1A Learner-educator ratio: Primary school, 1996

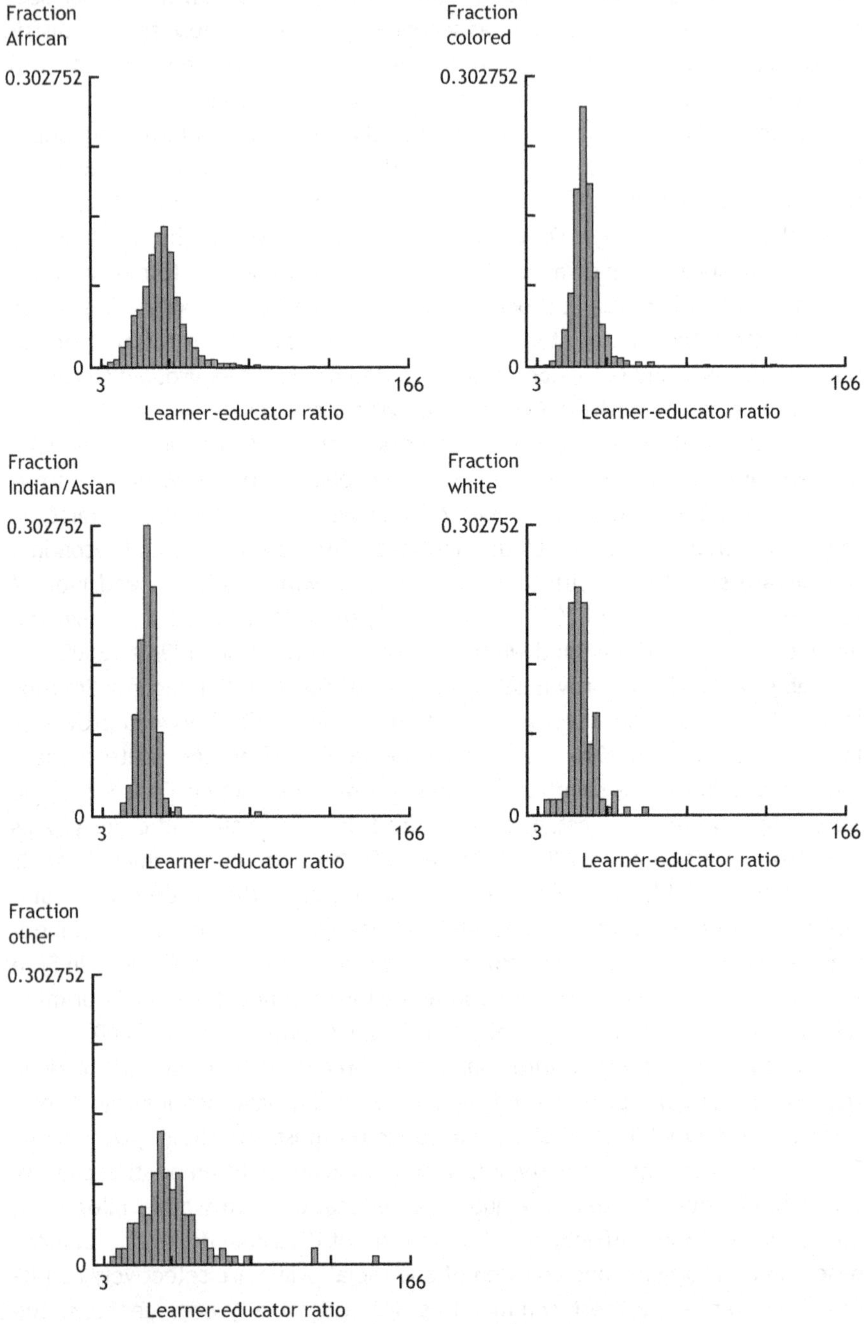

Source: Republic of South Africa, Department of Education (1996).

Figure 2.1B Learner-educator ratio: Primary school, 2000

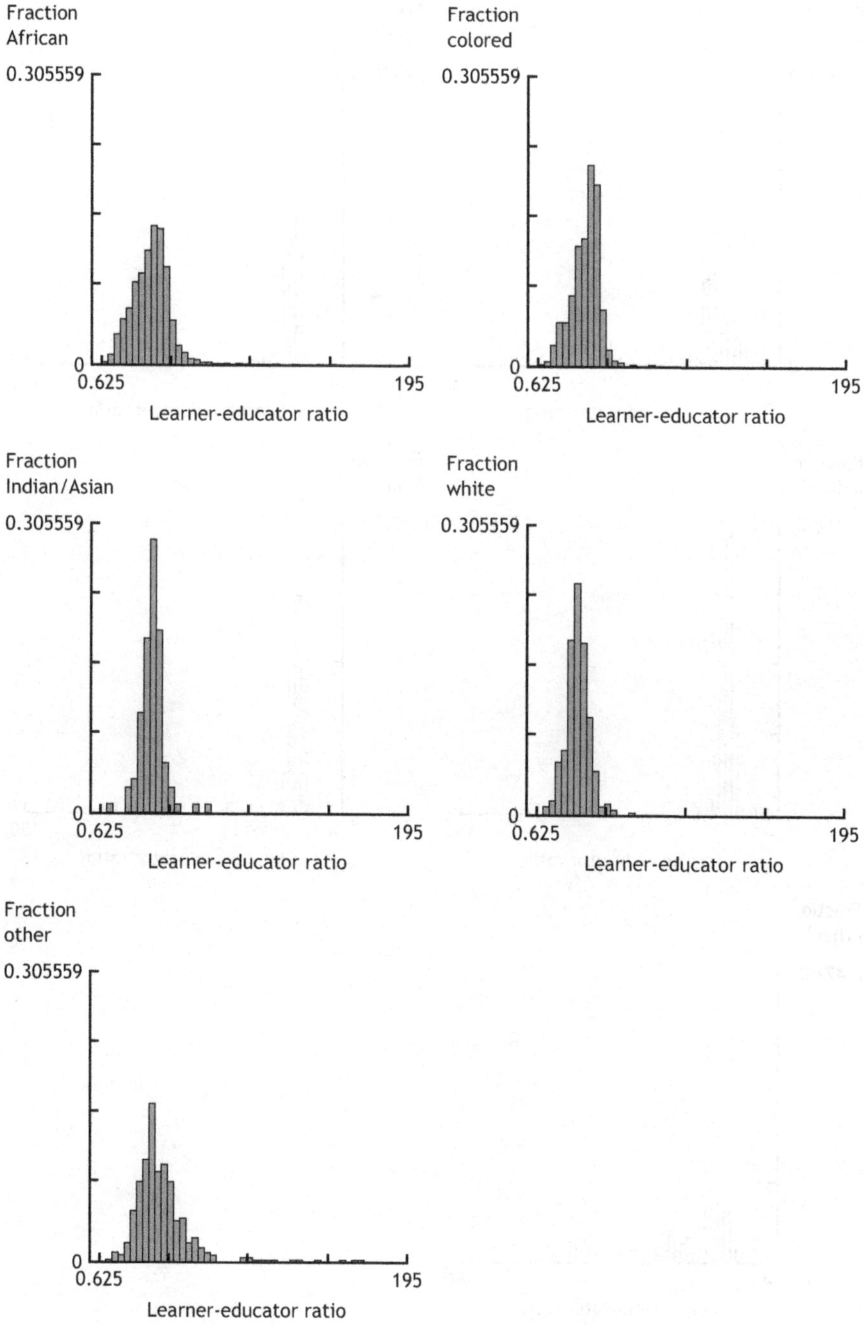

Source: Republic of South Africa, Department of Education (2000).

Figure 2.2A Learner-educator ratio: Secondary school, 1996

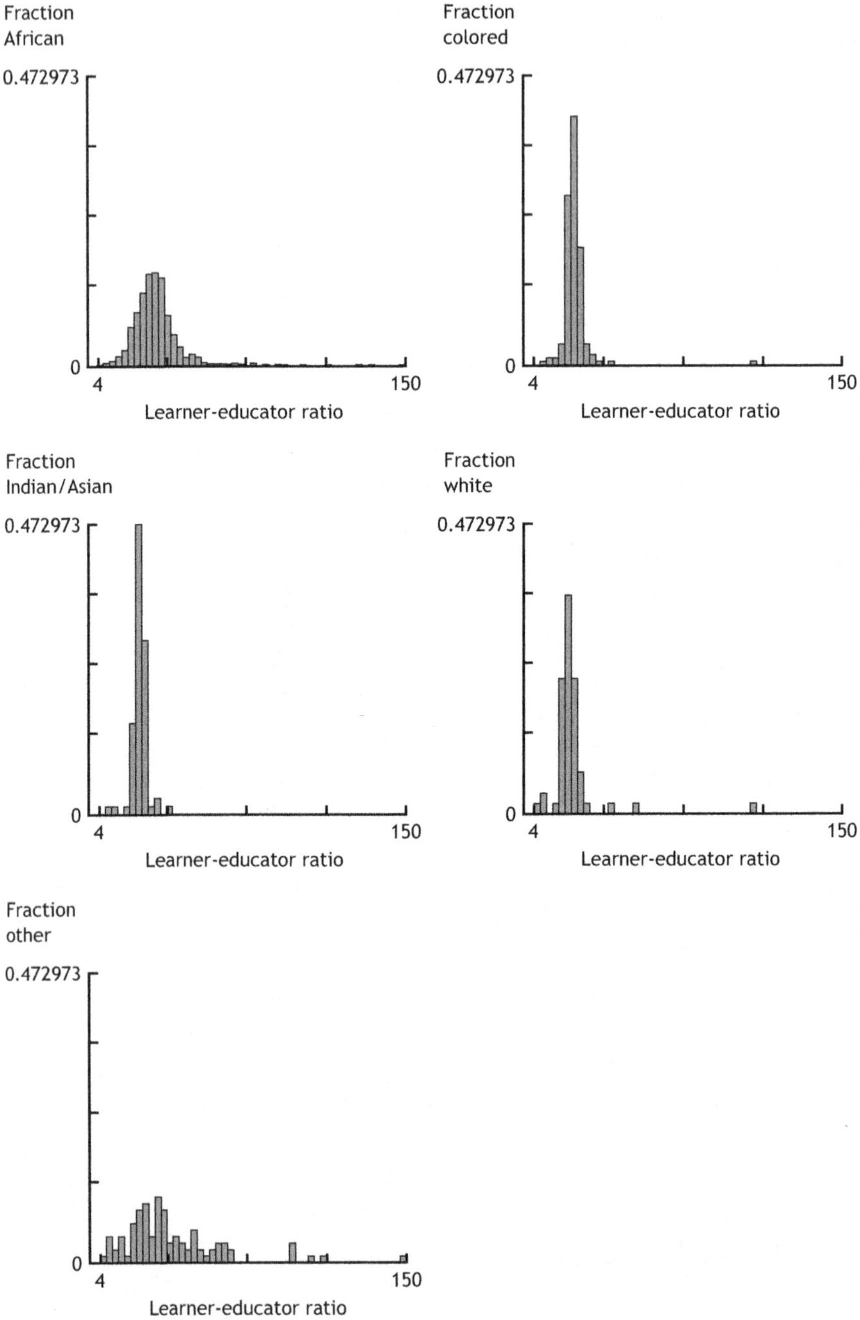

Source: Republic of South Africa, Department of Education (1996).

Figure 2.2B Learner-educator ratio: Secondary school, 2000

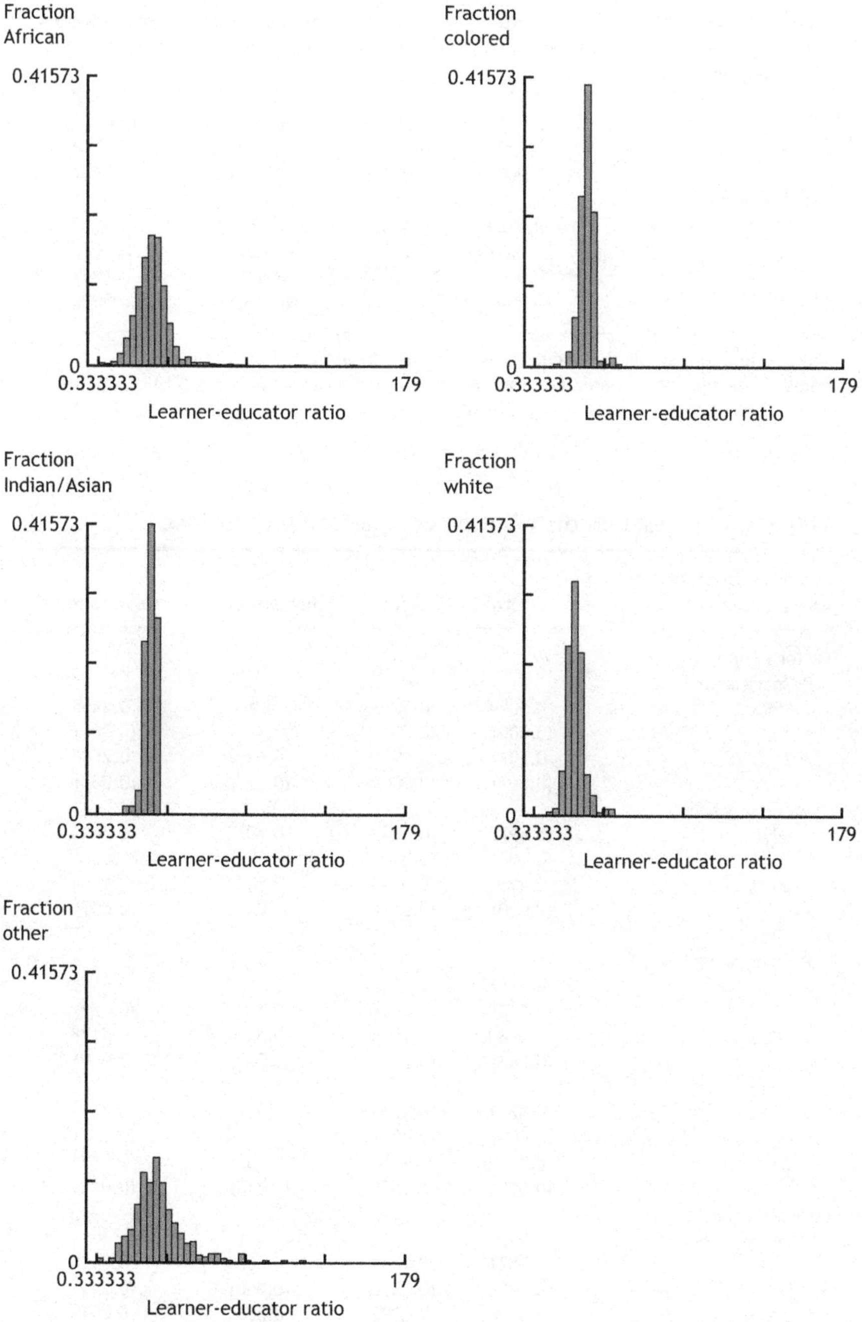

Source: Republic of South Africa, Department of Education (2000).

Table 2.3A Tests on distribution comparison

Population group, year	White	Colored	Indian/Asian	New schools
Primary school				
1996	0.5019	0.4185	0.5156	0.1348
	(0.000)	(0.000)	(0.000)	(0.026)
2000	0.3370	0.1279	0.1843	0.2208
	(0.000)	(0.000)	(0.001)	(0.000)
Secondary school				
1996	0.6729	0.6228	0.6677	0.2157
	(0.000)	(0.000)	(0.000)	(0.000)
2000	0.5202	0.2565	0.2710	0.1949
	(0.000)	(0.000)	(0.000)	(0.000)

Sources: Republic of South Africa, Department of Education (1996, 2000).
Notes: Numbers not in parentheses are *D*-values of Kolmogorov-Smirnov statistics, and the numbers in parentheses are *p*-values.

Table 2.3B Tests on distribution comparison by province

Province/population group, year	White	Colored	Indian/Asian	New schools
Eastern Cape				
Primary school				
1996	0.5074	0.5037	n.a.	0.3454
	(0.000)	(0.000)		(0.006)
2000	0.2917	0.1971	0.6399	0.2583
	(0.001)	(0.000)	(0.235)	(0.000)
Secondary school				
1996	0.6977	0.5803	0.7017	0.2643
	(0.002)	(0.000)	(0.598)	(0.035)
2000	0.4953	0.2194	0.5442	0.1564
	(0.000)	(0.067)	(0.877)	(0.007)
Free State				
Primary school				
1996	0.2152	0.1152	0.4504	0.3495
	(0.152)	(0.516)	(0.154)	(0.024)
2000	0.2140	0.1506	0.6553	0.4138
	(0.168)	(0.234)	(0.010)	(0.000)
Secondary school				
1996	0.6217	0.7205	0.9379	0.2531
	(0.000)	(0.001)	(0.243)	(0.917)
2000	0.5099	0.3220	0.9634	0.6391
	(0.000)	(0.055)	(0.216)	(0.000)
KwaZulu-Natal				
Primary school				
1996	0.5521	0.1284	0.6604	0.2115
	(0.001)	(0.331)	(0.000)	(0.549)
2000	0.5798	0.0792	0.3036	0.2013
	(0.000)	(0.628)	(0.000)	(0.000)

Table 2.3B Continued

Province/population group, year	White	Colored	Indian/Asian	New schools
Secondary school				
1996	0.7227	0.6012	0.6141	0.2212
	(0.000)	(0.000)	(0.000)	(0.873)
2000	0.6592	0.2141	0.4566	0.2577
	(0.000)	(0.152)	(0.000)	(0.000)
Northern Province				
Primary school				
1996	0.7360	0.5039	0.9753	0.2545
	(0.000)	(0.148)	(0.201)	(0.010)
2000	0.2988	0.3184	0.7742	0.4093
	(0.005)	(0.838)	(0.465)	(0.000)
Secondary school				
1996	0.9194	n.a.	0.9964	0.2582
	(0.000)		(0.183)	(0.004)
2000	0.4068	0.4549	n.a.	0.2743
	(0.014)	(0.662)		(0.000)
North West				
Primary school				
1996	0.5789	0.2244	0.3581	0.2008
	(0.032)	(0.587)	(0.218)	(0.382)
2000	0.2152	0.3739	0.2901	0.2875
	(0.576)	(0.022)	(0.260)	(0.001)
Secondary school				
1996	0.8347	0.5785	0.8760	0.3361
	(0.001)	(0.829)	(0.319)	(0.391)
2000	0.5670	0.7050	0.4330	0.2160
	(0.000)	(0.154)	(0.729)	(0.493)
Western Cape				
Primary school				
1996	0.8714	0.7492	0.9302	0.5168
	(0.000)	(0.000)	(0.001)	(0.011)
2000	0.7448	0.4732	0.7778	0.3333
	(0.000)	(0.000)	(0.024)	(0.030)
Secondary school				
1996	0.9375	0.8548	0.9688	0.5417
	(0.000)	(0.000)	(0.025)	(0.253)
2000	0.8141	0.3774	0.3182	0.1773
	(0.000)	(0.000)	(0.871)	(0.923)

Sources: Republic of South Africa, Department of Education (1996, 2000).

Notes: Numbers not in parentheses are *D*-values of Kolmogorov-Smirnov statistics, and the numbers in parentheses are *p*-values. n.a. means not available.

former population group (per the 2000 SRN) still represents the majority of the racial group at the school level.

Learner-Educator Changes

To cope with variations in the slope parameter across population groups and regions, and possibly at various levels of learner changes, I sort them by population groups, to the extent that the sample size of each group can permit analysis. In preliminary analyses, I found that if I used primary and secondary schools separately, sample sizes for non-African schools at the provincial levels became too small.[9]

Figure 2.3 depicts relationships between changes in primary-school educators and learners in 1996-2000 for all races and for different racial groups. The samples I use in this exercise are constructed as follows. Among schools that are successfully matched between SRN 1996 and 2000 by EMIS codes and province codes, I use only those classified by funding type as state or state-aided in 1996, those that show learner changes in the range of -1,000 to 1,000, and those that show educator changes in the range of -100 to 100. I dropped observations with missing values for the total number of educators in 1996 or 2000. Primary schools include normal primary (grades 1-7), junior primary (grades 1-4), and senior primary (grades 5-7) in the 1996 survey. Similarly, secondary schools include secondary (grades 8-12), junior secondary (grades 8-10), and senior secondary (grades 11-12) in 1996. If schools changed the range of grades offered during the period, they experienced large increases or decreases in learners.

In Figure 2.3 the relationship is close to linear but shows a slightly convex shape. However, it is asymmetric between the point at which the number of learners increases and the point at which it decreases. The response of educators to increases in the number of learners is larger than that to

---

[9] In nonparametric analysis of cross-provincial differences among African schools (Eastern Cape, Free State, KwaZulu-Natal, Northern Province (Limpopo), North West, and Western Cape), I used the same criteria used in Figures 2.1 and 2.2. In all provinces, changes in educators responded to those in learners positively. Though we find some variations in the slope across provinces, the magnitude is very small among African schools. Strong nonlinearity cannot be detected in these figures. However, it seems that while some provinces, such as Eastern Cape, Northern Province, and North West, did not experience large changes in learners at the school level, other provinces, such as Free State, KwaZulu-Natal, and Western Cape, have gone through large changes in number of learners.

For African secondary schools by province, it is also found that changes in educators responded to those in learners positively in all provinces. However, except in KwaZulu-Natal, the variations in educator change seem to be larger in this case than those for primary schools. In this sense, the equity-improving interventions were larger in secondary schools, and thus worked to narrow the gaps across schools.

Figure 2.3A Dynamic changes: Primary school

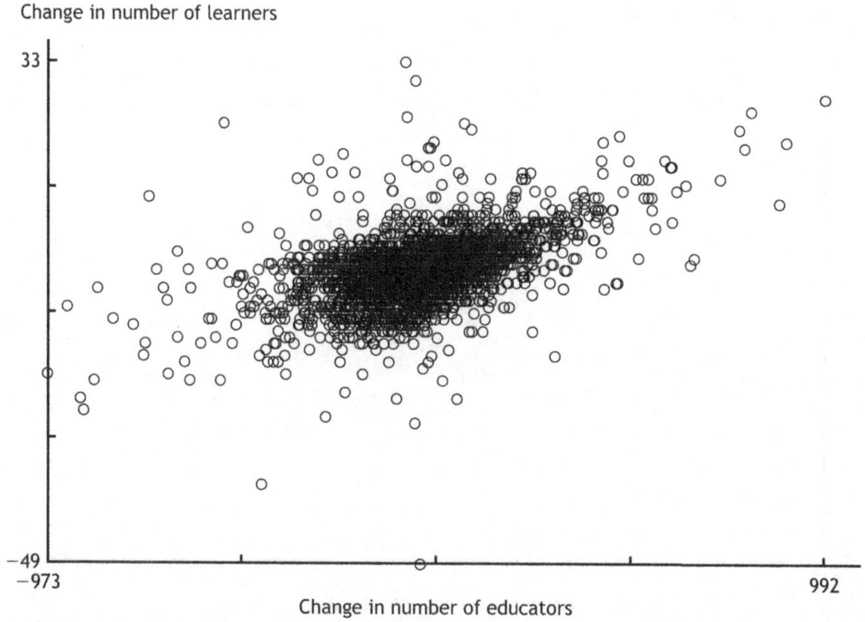

Sources: Republic of South Africa, Department of Education (1996, 2000).

Figure 2.3B Dynamic changes: Primary school, African

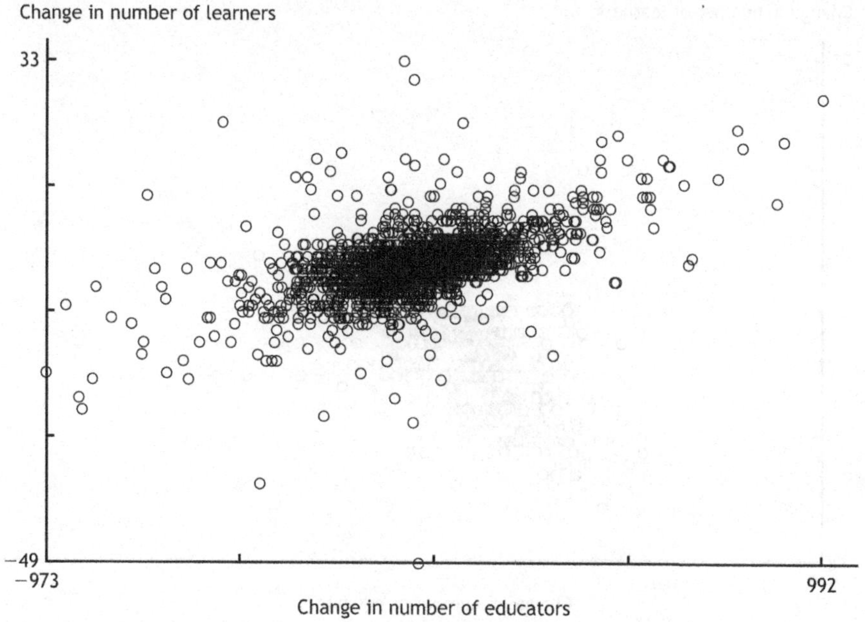

Sources: Republic of South Africa, Department of Education (1996, 2000).

Figure 2.3C Dynamic changes: Primary school, white

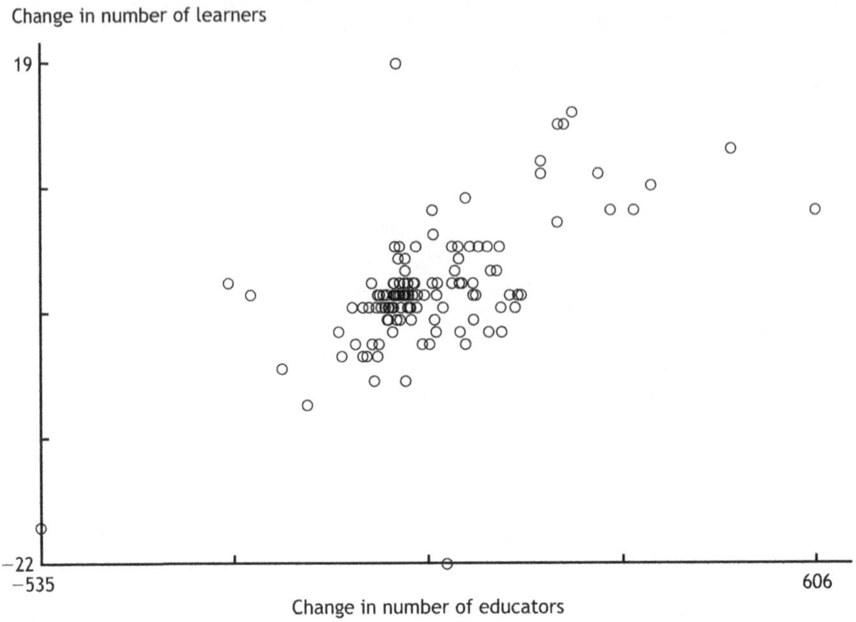

Sources: Republic of South Africa, Department of Education (1996, 2000).

Figure 2.3D Dynamic changes: Primary school, colored

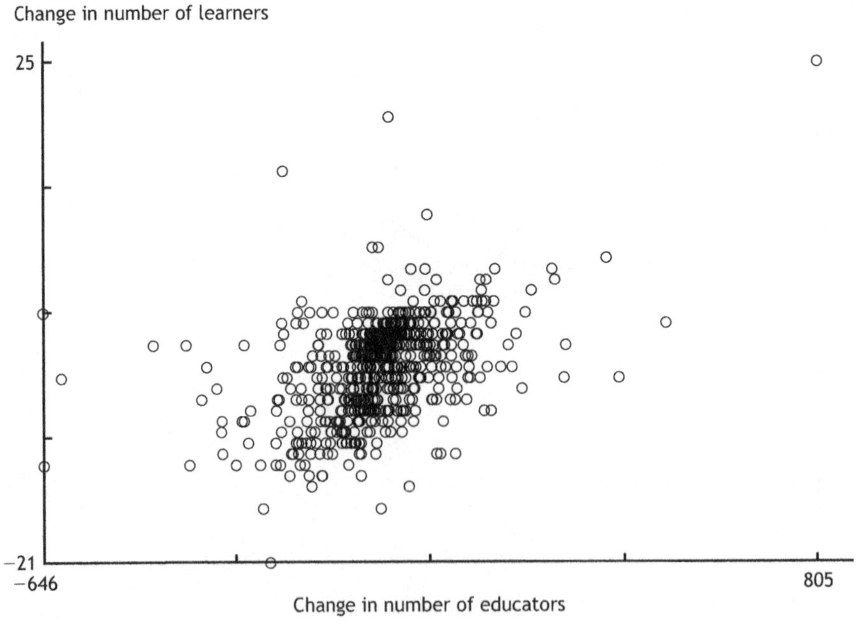

Sources: Republic of South Africa, Department of Education (1996, 2000).

Figure 2.3E Dynamic changes: Primary school, Indian/Asian

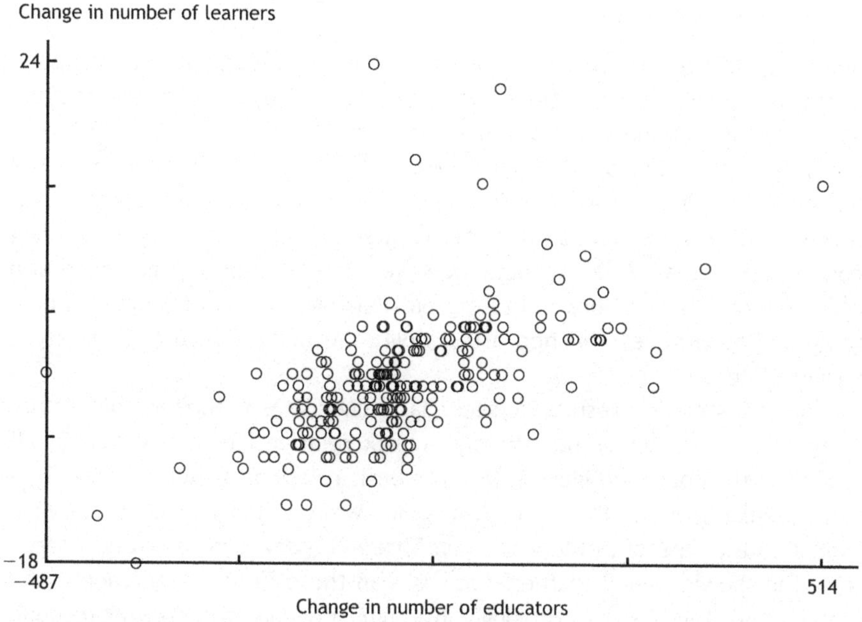

Sources: Republic of South Africa, Department of Education (1996, 2000).

Figure 2.3F Dynamic changes: Primary school, new schools

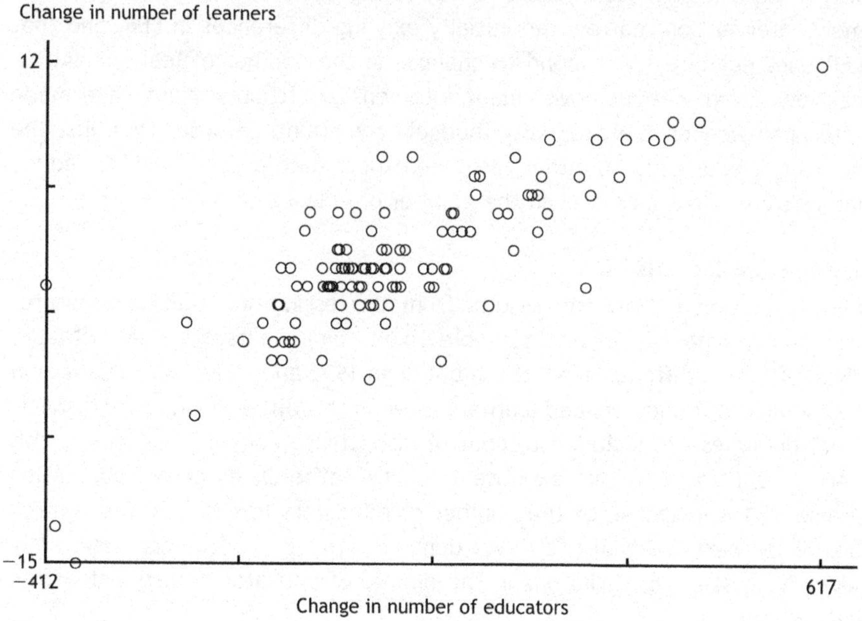

Sources: Republic of South Africa, Department of Education (1996, 2000).

decreases in the number of learners. In Figure 2.3B, in African schools, we have the same observations. However, for white, colored, and Indian/ Asian schools, nonlinearity becomes very strong (Figures 2.3C, 2.3D, and 2.3E). In white schools, while most observations show small changes in the number of learners, the overall shape is kinked with concavity (that is, there is slower adjustment when the number of learners increases). Among colored and Indian/Asian schools, however, the relationship is kinked and convex. Most observations in these groups also show small changes. In new schools that were established after 1994, the plot of results is nearly a straight line.

Figure 2.4 depicts results for secondary schools. As in the case of primary schools, a nearly linear but slightly convex relationship is observed in all schools in the country (Figure 2.4A). The basic relationship holds among African schools (Figure 2.4B). Figure 2.4C shows white schools: it looks strikingly similar to the case of primary schools. Though observations are less concentrated in showing small learner changes than those for primary schools, the shape is kinked and concave. Strikingly, the number of educators does not respond significantly to large changes in the number of learners, but it does respond to small changes.

One interesting observation from all these figures is that the cross-school variations in educator changes are quite large. The variations are large even with small changes in learners. One way to explain this finding is that government interventions narrow the initially existing differences in LER, and that LER does not directly respond to changes in the number of learners. Alternatively, even without government intervention, schools might have made efforts to weaken their liquidity (budget) constraints in order to adjust the number of educators. In either case, we expect that larger 1996 LERs induce larger subsequent increases in the number of educators.

Estimation Results

In this section I show the results from the estimation that incorporates community-school level unobservable fixed components. To deal with the fixed effects, I difference out those between 1996 and 2000, using changes in the number of educators and learners. Even in this differenced form, district-level dummies are included to control districtwise common changes in this period. Our focus in this exercise is on the differences across population groups in the response of the number of educators to changes in the number of learners. With district-level dummies, this procedure can essentially identify cross-group variations in the degree of educator adjustment within each district.

Figure 2.4A Dynamic changes: Secondary school

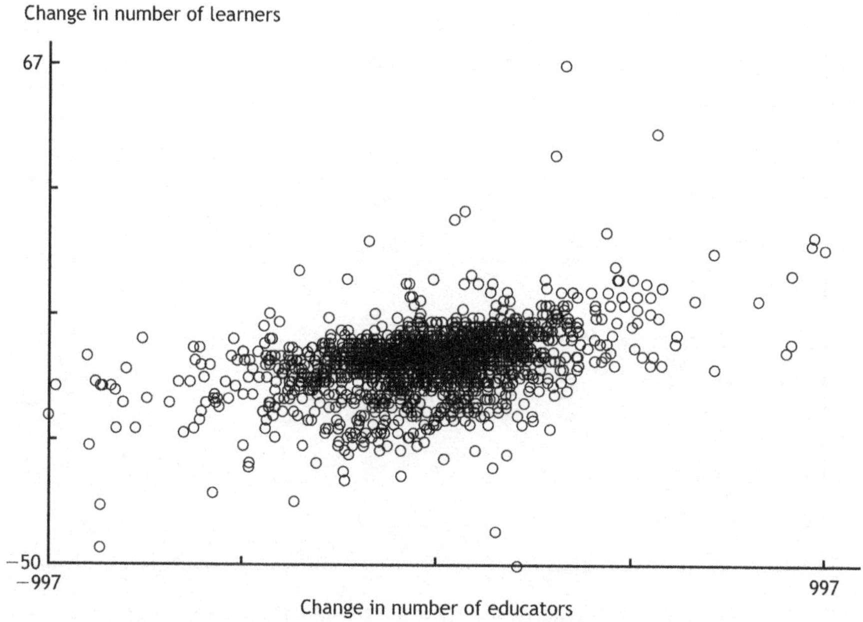

Sources: Republic of South Africa, Department of Education (1996, 2000).

Figure 2.4B Dynamic changes: Secondary school, African

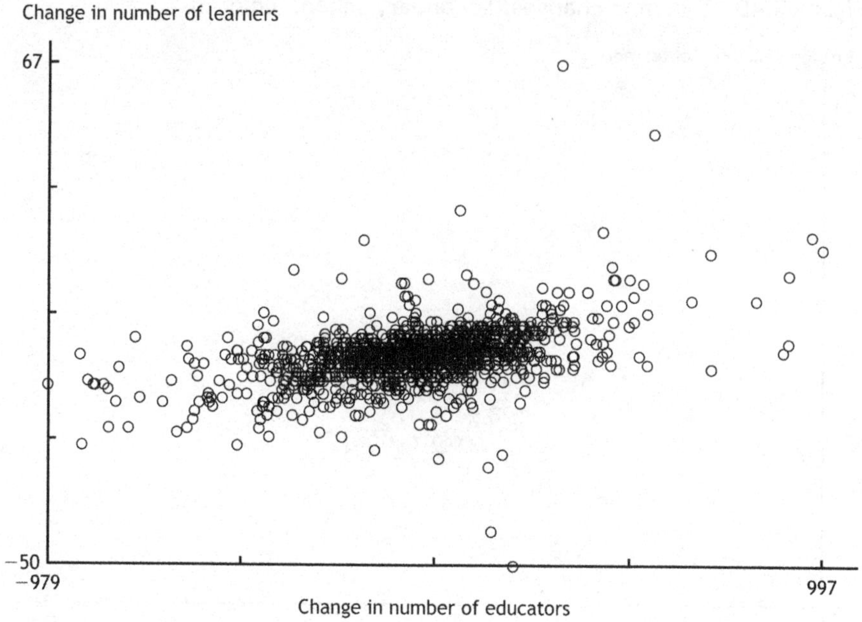

Sources: Republic of South Africa, Department of Education (1996, 2000).

Figure 2.4C Dynamic changes: Secondary school, white

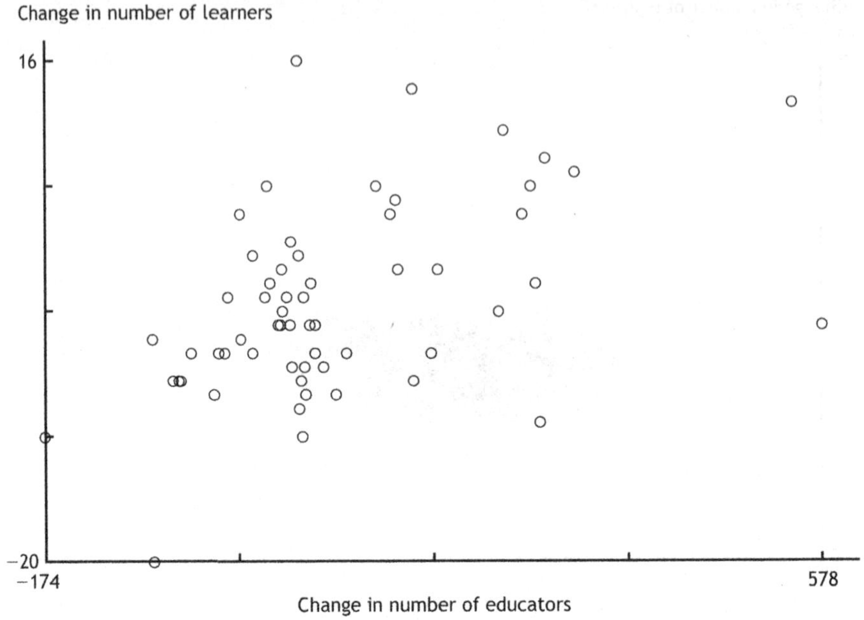

Sources: Republic of South Africa, Department of Education (1996, 2000).

Figure 2.4D Dynamic changes: Secondary school, colored

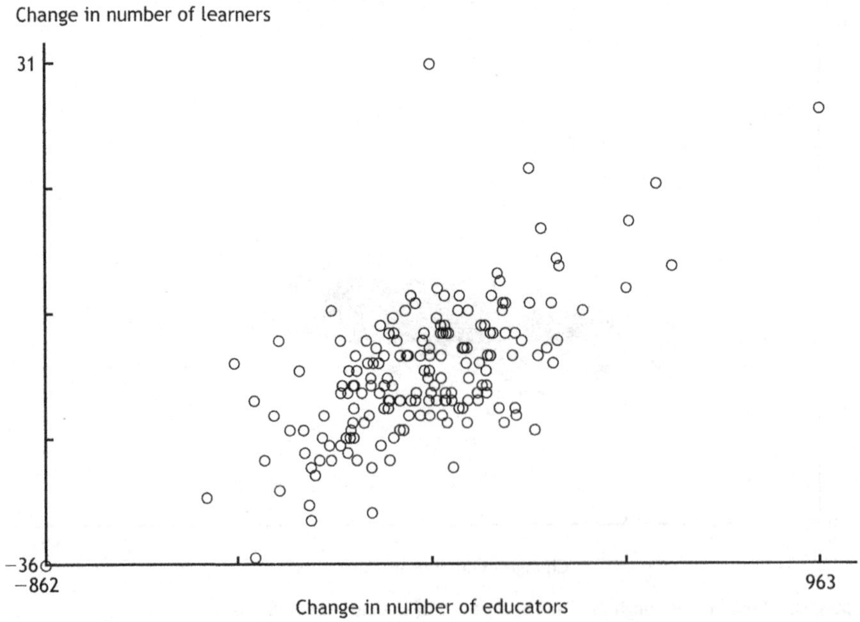

Sources: Republic of South Africa, Department of Education (1996, 2000).

Figure 2.4E Dynamic changes: Secondary school, Indian/Asian

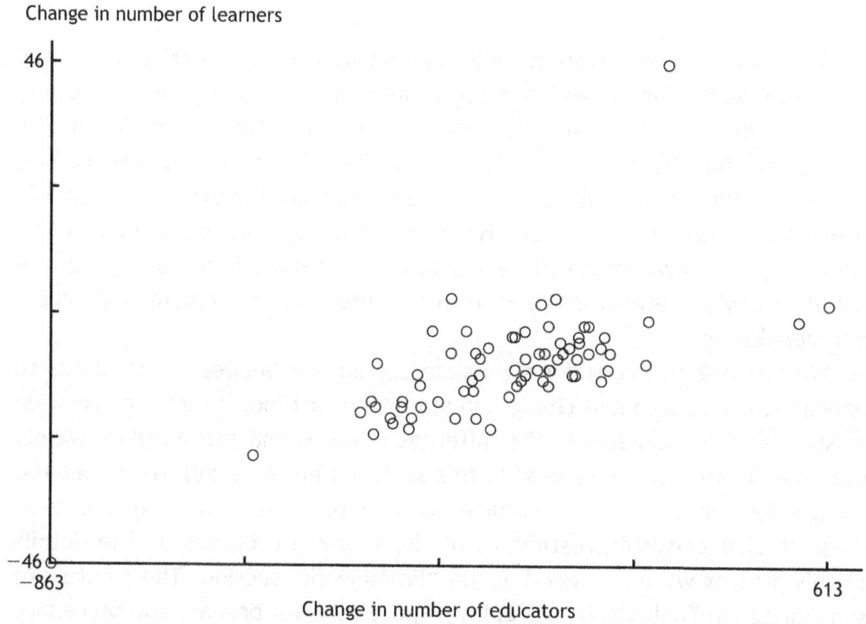

Sources: Republic of South Africa, Department of Education (1996, 2000).

Figure 2.4F Dynamic changes: Secondary school, new schools

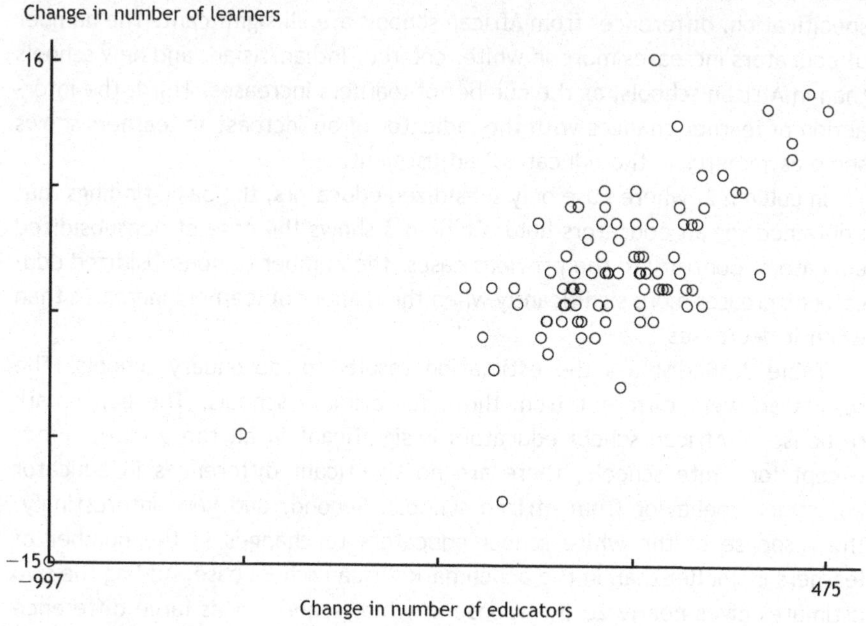

Sources: Republic of South Africa, Department of Education (1996, 2000).

This identification strategy calls for attention to the spatial residential pattern in South Africa, which is segregated by racial group. In the former homeland districts, for example, most of the communities are predominantly African, so that there exist few formerly white schools in such regions. This situation makes it difficult to identify gaps in school behavior between formerly African and white schools. However, provided that socioeconomic circumstances are diverse in different districts, it is more important to control the districtwise heterogeneity in terms of learners' movement and school decisionmaking.

We also need to consider a possible correlation between past shocks to educators and subsequent changes in learners over time. If such a correlation exists, the OLS estimates in the differenced forms will provide downwardly biased estimates of the slopes. In this section I not only difference out the fixed effects but also use instrumental variables available from the 1996 data, so that consistent estimates of the slopes are obtained. The details of this process were discussed in the "Framework" section. The results are summarized in Tables 2.4A and 2.4B, respectively, for primary and secondary schools. I also decompose the educators into two categories: subsidized and nonsubsidized.

Column 1 in Table 2.4A shows the response of the number of all educators to changes in the number of learners. First, the number of educators responds positively to an increase in the number of learners. Second, in this basic specification, differences from African schools are all significant. The number of educators increases more in white, colored, Indian/Asian, and new schools than in African schools, as the number of learners increases. Third, the interaction of learner changes with the indicator of an increase in learners shows some asymmetry in the educators' adjustment.

In column 2, where I use only subsidized educators, the basic findings that I obtained for all educators hold. Column 3 shows the case of nonsubsidized educators. Contrary to the previous cases, the number of nonsubsidized educators increases more significantly when the number of learners increases than when it decreases.

Table 2.4B displays the estimation results for secondary schools. The results are very different from those for primary schools. The benchmark response of African school educators is significant in all three cases. First, except for white schools, there are no significant differences in educator adjustment behavior from African schools. Second, and very interestingly, the response of the white school educators to changes in the number of learners is smaller than in the benchmark African school case. Adding the two estimates gives nearly zero response in white schools. This large difference from the primary school case suggests that at the secondary level the number

Table 2.4A Dynamic response: Public primary schools

Explanatory variable	All educators (1)	Subsidized (2)	Nonsubsidized (3)
Change in number of learners	0.0068	0.0065	0.0003
	(3.13)	(3.14)	(1.04)
× White	0.0107	0.0044	0.0063
	(2.89)	(1.05)	(3.41)
× Colored	0.0018	0.0018	-0.00007
	(0.61)	(0.69)	(0.13)
× Indian/Asian	0.0094	0.0079	0.0015
	(4.75)	(4.26)	(2.04)
× New schools	0.0167	0.0159	0.0008
	(1.72)	(1.62)	(0.57)
× Indicator: increase	0.0122	0.0120	0.0003
	(3.96)	(3.90)	(0.54)
Number of observations	4,663	4,663	4,663
R^2	0.3823	0.4028	0.1666

Sources: Republic of South Africa, Department of Education (1996, 2000).
Notes: The dependent variable is change in number of educators. The numbers in parentheses are absolute *t*-values. All specifications include race and district dummies. Robust standard errors are used with district-level clusters.

Table 2.4B Dynamic response: Public secondary schools

Explanatory variable	All educators (1)	Subsidized (2)	Nonsubsidized (3)
Change in number of learners	0.0087	0.0081	0.0005
	(4.60)	(4.35)	(1.53)
× White	-0.0069	-0.0087	0.0018
	(2.51)	(2.98)	(1.71)
× Colored	0.0133	0.0126	0.0007
	(3.23)	(2.83)	(0.84)
× Indian/Asian	0.0112	0.0096	0.0017
	(1.25)	(1.06)	(1.67)
× New schools	0.0023	0.0015	0.0008
	(0.99)	(0.63)	(1.14)
× Indicator: increase	0.0080	0.0079	0.00005
	(2.36)	(2.26)	(0.06)
Number of observations	1,646	1,646	1,646
R^2	0.5209	0.5300	0.3658

Sources: Republic of South Africa, Department of Education (1996, 2000).
Notes: The dependent variable is change in number of educators. The numbers in parentheses are absolute *t*-values. All specifications include race and district dummies. Robust standard errors are used with district-level clusters.

of educators has already been close to the optimal level among white schools, so that even in response to relatively small changes in the number of learners, schools do not adjust the number of educators significantly. Third, colored schools show stronger responses than African schools. There seem to be larger behavioral variations across different population groups in secondary schools than in primary schools. Fourth, except for the case of nonsubsidized educators, changes in the number of educators are larger when the number of learners increases than when it decreases.

Summary

The empirical results show that opportunities for education in public schools are still unequal between African and white children in South Africa, even after the end of apartheid. The LERs in public primary and secondary schools differ statistically between African and white groups. During the period 1996–2000, overall differences in the distribution of LERs have not changed, and in some cases the gaps have been even reinforced for secondary schools. The resulting inequality in opportunities for education could lead to persistent inequality in labor markets and earning opportunities since the quantity and quality of education crucially determine labor market outcomes.

The dynamics of school education also demonstrate strong inequity between population groups. The number of educators responds to changes in the number of learners in all population groups at the primary school level. However, the adjustment in the number of educators is significantly larger for formerly white, colored, Indian/Asian, and new schools than African schools. On the other hand, at the secondary school level, the results do not display significant apartheid-type inequity. In the case of white schools, the number of educators does not respond to changes in the number of learners, probably because these schools have retained their initial superiority.

One possible reason why LERs have not converged even after the abolition of apartheid is that school fees charged at formerly white schools increased to prevent the entry of African children (Selod and Zenou 2003) (though the empirical analyses in this chapter do not address this proposition). This screening mechanism could partially explain changes in the number of learners and why LERs did not converge rapidly. It is also very difficult to obtain data on racial composition in each school.

Our empirical results call for stronger policy support for African primary schools and schoolchildren, which can contribute to the human-capital-based reduction of the poverty and inequality that have resulted from apartheid in South Africa.

CHAPTER 3

School Quality, Clustering, and Government Subsidy

Geography becomes critical when access to opportunities is distributed unevenly over space. For example, when good schools are concentrated in urban areas, one must live in these areas to have good educational opportunities and therefore good job prospects. In South Africa, which experienced nearly more than 40 years of apartheid, different population groups were segregated in separate residential areas with unequal access to education.[1] As a result, location was a critical factor. This chapter examines how spatial factors, highly correlated with historical factors, are determining school quality in post-apartheid South Africa.

Two factors are relevant to the way in which school quality is determined. First, the legacy of apartheid imposes historical constraints on the spatial distribution of income and population groups. Good schools are located in selected areas. This has maintained interracial diversity in access to good education, as well as racial and socioeconomic homogeneity within neighborhoods.[2]

Second, even if the mobility of populations was unrestricted after the abolition of apartheid, household-level financial constraints coupled with the imperfect credit market often prevent the poor from moving into those well-off areas that offer better educational opportunities. Thus the opportunity for better education is geographically correlated with land prices.[3] Even though African children can commute to formerly white schools, in so doing

This chapter is reproduced in part from an article in the journal *Economics of Education Review* (Yamauchi 2010).

[1] For accounts of the general situation in South African education, see Kriege et al. (1994); Crouch (1996); Bot, Wilson, and Dove (2000); Shindler and Fleisch (2007); van der Berg (2007); Bloch et al. (2008); and Fleisch (2008). As van der Berg (2007) argues, race still remains a major factor in explaining school performance.

[2] Yamauchi (2007a) discussed the importance of observed neighborhood heterogeneity for agents' learning about returns to schooling and deciding on schooling investment. Whether a society is heterogeneous or homogeneous has dynamic implications.

[3] This point has not yet been seriously examined, though casual observations support this proposition.

they incur additional transportation and time costs. Accordingly I explore the impact of apartheid on the spatial distribution of quality education under the post-apartheid regime, in which spatial mobility is legally unrestricted.[4]

This chapter asks how historical and location factors affect access to quality education in post-apartheid South Africa through the use of a unique database combining the 2002 school census and the Community Profile Database from the 2001 South African census. With the addition of GIS information, these data enable us to identify the location of a given school and to correlate that with local socioeconomic characteristics.

Given the abovementioned spatial dependence, the role of government subsidy is expected to be significant in creating equitable and equal access to education. I assess to what extent government subsidy disconnects the linkage between local resources and school quality, given that school fee determines school quality. For this purpose, I use school finance data from the province of KwaZulu-Natal to analyze the dependence of school quality, measured by the LER, on school fee and government subsidy.

Selod and Zenou (2003) examined the role of school fees in screening children from different backgrounds in a spatial model, showing that whites tend to overprice education in order to limit the numbers of African learners. It is likely that a high school fee supports high school quality even in South African public schools, as well as keeping the community and schools racially homogeneous. This chapter also provides some insight into this question.

The chapter is organized as follows. The section "Dependence of School Quality on Local Resources" discusses how school quality (inputs) can depend on local resources in South Africa. The following section describes the empirical framework and data used in the analysis.

Empirical results are summarized in the next section. First, some key spatial features of school fee distributions and population group compositions in South Africa are demonstrated and linked with the history of apartheid. School fees are significantly higher among formerly non-African schools and in predominantly white areas.

Second, while local population-group composition and former apartheid departments of education still influence the way in which school fees (and thus school quality) are determined for local public schools, the role of local income opportunity is also significant, especially in large cities. Third,

---

[4] Chapter 2 examined how LERs changed between 1996 and 2000, splitting the sample into formerly African, white, colored, and Indian/Asian schools. I showed that the change in the number of educators in response to a change in the number of learners is smaller in formerly African schools than in formerly white schools. This finding implies that the former group has been more likely to face financial constraints.

evidence from KwaZulu-Natal shows that school fees and per-learner government subsidies improve school quality, decreasing the LER and implying that more progressive allocation of subsidies can improve the quality of schools located in under-resourced communities. Policy implications are discussed in the final section.

Dependence of School Quality on Local Resources

School quality is a function of school inputs, which in the context of South Africa are determined by local resource availability (through school fees) and government subsidy. Here "school quality" does not mean learning achievements or educational outcomes. We assume that a given outcome is a function of not only school quality (inputs)—including the availability of qualified teaching staff—but also of learners' family backgrounds and their own efforts and ability. This chapter focuses on the resources available to schools.

Distinguishing between school inputs and educational outcomes is important. To analyze the determinants of educational outcomes, it is necessary to use some outcome measures such as test scores at the individual level or school averages. Qualified empirical analyses prove significant causal effects of school inputs on achievement (for example, Card and Krueger 1996; Angrist and Lavy 1999; Case and Deaton 1999; Krueger 1999; Hoxby 2000; Dustman, Rajah, and Soest 2003), though the literature has in general drawn mixed conclusions (Hanushek 1998), and causality seems to depend on subjects (Steele, Vignoles, and Jenkins 2007).

In the context of South Africa, Case and Deaton (1999) show that school resources, measured by LER, can explain test scores using variations in the ratio from that under apartheid.

More directly van der Berg (2007) used matriculation test pass rates to analyze the effects of school resources and socioeconomic factors on learners' learning performance. School fees, LER, and average teacher salary significantly influence the matriculation pass rate. Interestingly, former departments also have a significant effect on the rate. However, if the sample is restricted to formerly African schools, LER loses its statistical significance, implying that resource variations within this group are not relatively large. The level of school fees, correlated with local socioeconomic factors (as discussed later), significantly explains the matriculation pass rate even within formerly African schools.[5]

[5] In his paper, van der Berg (2007) argues that historical factors, such as former departments, teacher quality, and school management, are more important than school resources in determining school performance. Former departments are clearly correlated with matriculation pass rates. This tendency did not change even with progressive changes in school resource allocation

The mobility of learners and the dynamic nature of human capital formation raise other concerns. Since learners, especially at the secondary level under the post-apartheid regime, can potentially choose their schools more freely, endogenous school choice (mobility across communities) can be an important factor in determining educational outcomes at the school level.[6] Similarly, since prior investments in human capital affect educational outcomes at later stages, schooling inputs and outcomes at the primary school level are expected to influence those at the secondary level.[7] While mobility of learners can potentially weaken the spatial correlation between local factors and school outcomes, the dynamic production of human capital can strengthen the correlation.

To understand the linkage between school quality and local resources, we need to know the roles of school governing bodies (SGBs). It is the SGB—a group consisting of the principal, teachers, community leaders, parents, and in some secondary schools, learners themselves—that sets school fees. Accordingly, the school fees charged represent the community's ability to pay for education.[8] SGBs are playing an even greater role now; under recently implemented funding reforms, provincial governments allocate school subsidies according to local poverty measures. To assess the quality of education, information on school fees charged by local public schools is used. In South Africa, school fees determine not only school quality but also the likelihood that residents will be able to afford investments in schooling.

Until recently, government educational subsidies in South Africa have been limited, so financing of schools relies heavily on the collection of school fees—in effect a user charge—from parents. As mentioned in paragraph 46 of the 1998 Norms and Standards for School Funding,

> Ironically, given the emphasis on redress and equity, the funding provisions of the Act appear to have worked thus far to the advantage of public schools patronized by middle-class and wealthy parents. The

---

under the post-apartheid regime. We argue that the ability to hire more qualified teachers depends on the community's income level (school fees), which is spatially clustered in today's South Africa.

[6] Van der Berg (2007) reports that learners do not systematically move to better-quality schools probably because of lack of information on school performance, and that the amount of movement to private schools is minor. However, this observation was based on Western Cape province, so it is difficult to generalize.

[7] In a slightly different context, but one highly relevant to this issue, Yamauchi (2008) showed significant effects of preschool nutrition intake (forming early-childhood human capital) on schooling outcomes.

[8] See the 1998 Norms and Standards for School Funding (Republic of South Africa 1998), which was announced in response to the South African School Act (Republic of South Africa 1996b).

> apartheid regime favored such communities with high-quality facilities, equipment and resources. Vigorous fund-raising by parent bodies, including commercial sponsorships and fee income, have enabled many such schools to add to their facilities, equipment and learning resources, and expand their range of cultural and sporting activities. Since 1995, when such schools have been required to down-size their staff establishments, many have been able to recruit additional staff on governing body contracts, paid from the school fund.

As discussed in the introduction to this chapter, local resource availability is determined by historical and spatial factors, which are correlated in the current empirical context, given limited government subsidy. Choice of residential area is limited even now, so schools that are locally available to African children are largely formerly African institutions, many of which were historically disadvantaged and remain so. Schools in well-off areas can charge higher school fees, which not only finance school inputs but also allow them to avoid the enrollment of children from low-income families.

A school fee represents the community's capability to finance local public education. Yamauchi and Nishiyama (2005) analyzed the effect of local income distribution on the determination of school fees, showing that inequality decreases the level of school fee. Thus low-income groups in a community pull down school fees, an outcome that decreases school quality for all children in the community.[9]

If school inputs depend on local resources, to what extent does government subsidy disconnect the linkage between local resources and school quality? How effectively can progressive subsidy change the linkage between school quality and historically constrained local resource availability? In this analysis, I use LER as a measure of school quality (resource) to explore how local resources, approximated by school fees, and government subsidy can jointly determine school quality.

There is a potential substitution (trade-off) between local and government resources, both of which determine school inputs. If government subsidy completely equalizes unequal local endowments, school quality no longer depends on local resources. From a policy perspective, we are interested in knowing how differentially elastically our measure of school quality (LER) can change in response to changes in school fees versus government subsidy. In the following sections, we discuss the empirical framework, data, and results.

---

[9] In different contexts, Foster and Rosenzweig (2001) and Chattopadhyay and Duflo (2004) show the importance of local governance in public investment decisionmaking.

Empirical Framework and Data

School Fees

To assess the effects of historical and spatial factors on school quality, we estimate the following equation in which the log of school fee represents school quality:

$$\ln p_{jkt} = \alpha + x'_{kt\text{-}s}\beta_1 + z'_{jk}\beta_2 + \varepsilon_{jkt}, \qquad (3.1)$$

where $\ln p_{jkt}$ is the log of the school fee at school j in location (subplace) k at year t; $x_{kt\text{-}s}$ is location factors such as local population composition and economic conditions at s years prior to t; z_{jk} is historical factors at school j, such as the former department; and ε_{jkt} is an error term. Officially, a subplace is defined as the smallest geographic unit available from the census, by which we can identify the location as well as its characteristics. The novel feature of this approach is that location factors are discovered from merging school data and geographic database by GIS.[10]

The data come from two different sources. Local characteristics are taken from the Census 2001 Community Profile Database (Statistics South Africa). This database provides distributions of socioeconomic characteristics in the 2001 census at the subplace level for the whole country. It covers, for example, education, labor force, migration, settlement types, and population group compositions.

GIS data available in school censuses can help identify in which subplace a school is located.[11] The school identification codes, EMIS, enable us to merge the Census 2001 subplace data and school censuses. School fees in 2001 are captured in the Annual School Survey 2002 (National Department of Education). The information on former education departments is available in the SRN 2000 (National Department of Education).

School Quality

To answer the question of how the government can improve school quality and support the poor with spatially targeted interventions, we estimate the following school production functions:

$$\Delta y_{jk} = \gamma_0 + \gamma_1 \ln p_{jkt} + \gamma_2 \ln g_{jkt} + z'_{jk}\zeta + \Delta\xi_j \qquad (3.2)$$

[10] In the estimation, spatial dependence is not explicitly identified in the error term, beyond allowing clustered correlations within each subplace (robust standard errors).

[11] Using the same datasets, Yamauchi and Nishiyama (2005) analyze the effect of local income distribution within a subplace on the determination of school fees in public schools therein.

and

$$\Delta Y_{jk} = \gamma_0 + \gamma_1 \ln p_{jkt} + \gamma_2 \ln g_{jkt} + \gamma_3 \Delta L_{jk} + \gamma_4 \ln p_{jkt} \Delta L_{jk} + \gamma_5 \ln g_{jkt} \Delta L_{jk} + z'_{jk}\zeta + \Delta\xi_j, \quad (3.3)$$

where Δ is the difference operator, Y_{jk} is the number of educators, L_{jk} is the number of learners, y_{jk} is the LER, and g_{jkt} is the per-learner subsidy from the government. Here z_{jk} includes indicators of former departments. In both specifications, we take the first difference between two periods to eliminate school- and location-specific unobserved fixed effects.

The LER is used as a measure of school quality. However, we also admit that this measure can only partially capture overall school quality, which is determined by such other measures as teaching facilities (classroom conditions) and quality of school administration. I constructed the LER from two school censuses in 1996 and 2000, which focus on school facilities.[12] Since the government subsidy allocation had in principle not changed before 2000, we assume that the subsidy reported for 2000 was basically applied to the period before 2000.

To supplement the limited number of subsidized educators, community members can collect school fees and employ educators privately. I therefore also test whether a change in the number of learners induces a change in the number of educators who are privately employed in the community.

If the government allocates subsidy more to disadvantaged schools (that is, a smaller number of educators relative to the number of learners), potential bias in γ_2 would be upward since differenced ξ_{jt} are positively correlated with per-learner subsidy g_{jkt}. On the other hand, if government subsidy allocation increases inequality in the number of educators, we expect a downward bias in the estimate. However, since fixed unobservables are already differenced out, the systematic component of endogenous subsidy allocation has no impact on our estimates.

Finally, the determination of per-learner subsidy is also of interest in the empirical analysis. Though one possible way to eliminate the bias mentioned earlier is to use instruments for g_{jkt}, we lack identifying instruments in the available data. Therefore I simply examine the effects of school fees, the initial LER, former departments, and school type and location fixed effects.

---

[12] Since measurement errors are reported on number of learners in the Annual School Surveys, we decided to use the 1996 and 2000 SRNs. These have a simplified questionnaire structure focusing on school facility information. Therefore, they are likely to have smaller measurement errors.

For this analysis, I use school and community information from the province of KwaZulu-Natal. School information comes from the Annual School Survey 1999 (Department of Education) and the KwaZulu-Natal Department of Education's Norms and Standards database. The information on school fees in 1999 and 2000 is also from the KwaZulu-Natal Department of Education. In the province of KwaZulu-Natal, therefore, we can track dynamic changes in school fees to check the robustness of the principal findings.

To assess school quality, I use SRN 1996 and 2000 (National Department of Education), which focus on school facility information, making them suitable for computing changes in LERs and number of educators from 1996 to 2000.[13]

Data on government subsidy are from the KwaZulu-Natal Department of Education (Norms and Standards database). Current funding reforms in the South African public education system attempt to allocate more funding to poor schools and communities on the basis of a poverty ranking of schools and areas within each province. I use the information on actual funding during the period January-March 2000, before the implementation of the funding reforms, so that we can assume that it represents the status quo in the period prior to 2000.

Empirical Results

School Fees, Apartheid Education Departments, and School Neighborhoods

This section clarifies some features of the public education system in South Africa, using school fees as a proxy for school quality. We need to be aware of the history of modern South Africa, and of two factors in particular. The first is the segregation policy adopted in education under apartheid, by which population groups were separated from each other in various dimensions. In public education, different departments were responsible for different population groups, and children from different population groups were segregated in separate schools. The second factor is the spatial distribution of residential areas and school locations. Because of the segregation policy under apartheid, different population groups were not allowed to live in the same area. Thus formerly white schools are located in formerly white areas.

Figure 3.1 depicts the distribution of annual school fees charged for public schools in 2001 (the weight being number of learners). The mean school fee is 431.72 rand, while the median is 50 rand, which implies that

---

[13] In this analysis, we need information on school fees and government funding as key explanatory factors. Since the latter information is available only in the province of KwaZulu-Natal, we restrict our analysis to that province.

Figure 3.1 Distribution of log annual school fee

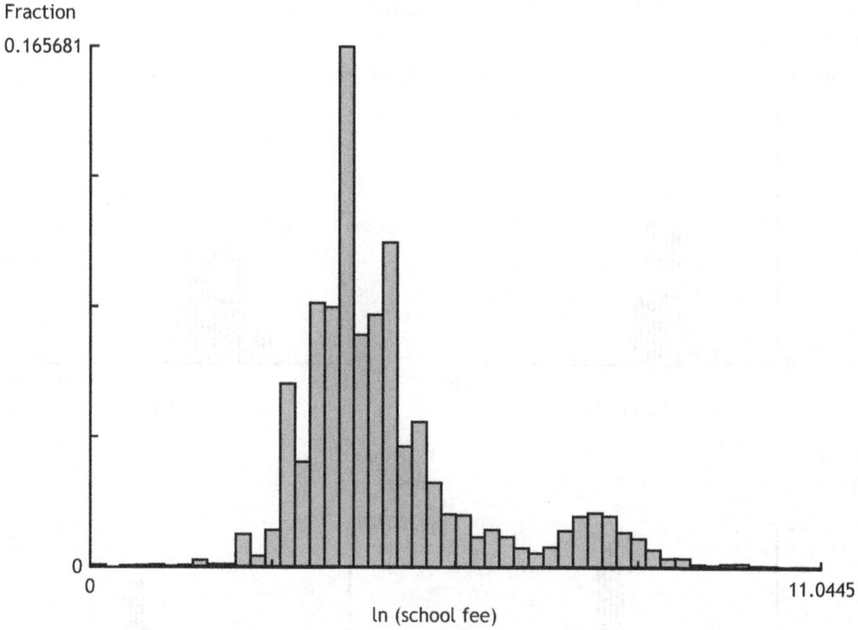

Source: Republic of South Africa, Department of Education (2002).

the distribution is highly skewed. Interestingly the graph exhibits a clear bimodal distribution, showing that a group of public schools charges higher fees than the majority. It is also possible that their locations have certain characteristics in common.

Figure 3.2 depicts school fee distributions for population groups defined by the former education departments, to illustrate the impact of apartheid on school fee distribution. In South Africa before 1994, the Department of Education and Culture's House of Assembly (HOA), House of Representatives (HOR), and House of Delegates (HOD) governed white, colored, and Indian/Asian schools, respectively. The Transvaal Education Department (TED) represented white schools in Gauteng province. Schools established after 1994 are categorized as a new group. These figures clearly show the importance of the historical influence of the former regime. Schools formerly under the control of HOA, HOR, HOD, and TED charged higher school fees than schools for other groups. The finding suggests that, given that school fees are positively correlated with school quality, formerly white, colored, and Indian/Asian schools provide higher-quality education than the majority of formerly African schools.

Figure 3.2 Former department groups and log annual school fee

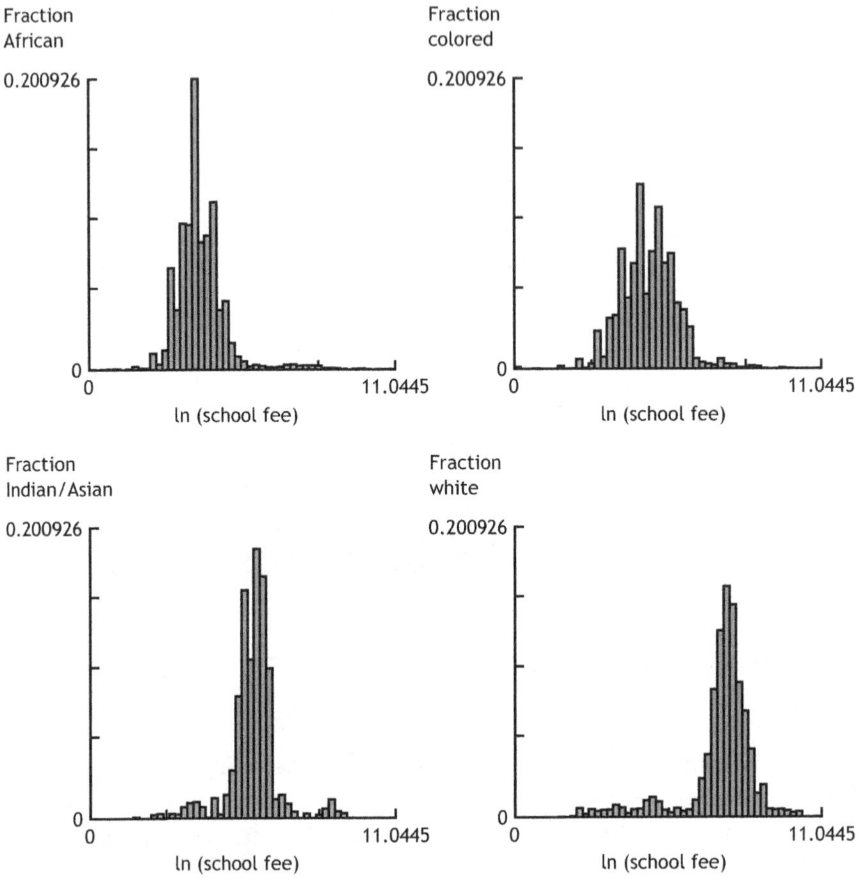

Sources: Republic of South Africa, Department of Education (2000, 2002).

Next, the relationship between former departments and population group composition in school neighborhoods is demonstrated. Table 3.1 shows the proportions of African, white, colored, and Indian/Asian populations in the census subplace of school location. Note that the population group compositions are computed from the Census 2001 Community Profile Database, whereas former departments are those under the pre-1994 apartheid regime.

It is interesting to confirm that formerly white schools are located in subplaces where the white population is still the majority. Similarly, formerly Indian/Asian schools are in subplaces where the majority population is Indian/Asian. Formerly colored schools are in colored and white-dominated

Table 3.1 Population group compositions in school neighborhoods

Local population group composition	Number of observations	Mean	Standard deviation	Minimum	Maximum
Primary schools					
African					
Proportion African	13,359	0.9442374	0.1376764	0	1
Proportion white	13,359	0.0386878	0.1017163	0	1
Proportion colored	13,359	0.0144011	0.0679492	0	0.9874739
Proportion Indian/Asian	13,359	0.0026737	0.0303421	0	0.9637306
White					
Proportion African	983	0.3257602	0.3057272	0	1
Proportion white	983	0.5418614	0.3102345	0	0.9710921
Proportion colored	983	0.1059982	0.2009087	0	0.9740787
Proportion Indian/Asian	983	0.0263803	0.0571967	0	0.6671807
Colored					
Proportion African	1,378	0.2563067	0.3321149	0	1
Proportion white	1,378	0.1023137	0.1501915	0	1
Proportion colored	1,378	0.6316433	0.3432725	0	1
Proportion India/Asian	1,378	0.0097363	0.0498904	0	0.8288214
Indian/Asian					
Proportion African	331	0.3177387	0.3230634	0.0034247	1
Proportion white	331	0.0607398	0.1713729	0	0.8977141
Proportion colored	331	0.0482009	0.1383091	0	0.9862803
Proportion Indian/Asian	331	0.5733206	0.3796239	0	0.9885057
Secondary schools					
African					
Proportion African	4,475	0.9604805	0.1489296	0	1
Proportion white	4,475	0.0249173	0.1126637	0	1
Proportion colored	4,475	0.0100202	0.0649181	0	0.9798253
Proportion Indian/Asian	4,475	0.004582	0.0447487	0	0.9756098
White					
Proportion African	439	0.281697	0.2692092	0	1
Proportion white	439	0.5917889	0.2862688	0	1
Proportion colored	439	0.0990783	0.1792077	0	0.9653361
Proportion Indian/Asian	439	0.0274358	0.0466701	0	0.3062209
Colored					
Proportion African	270	0.1625991	0.2753492	0	1
Proportion white	270	0.1162389	0.2441152	0	0.9690049
Proportion colored	270	0.7080628	0.3575151	0	0.9976985
Proportion Indian/Asian	270	0.0130991	0.0312058	0	0.3442088
Indian/Asian					
Proportion African	102	0.1836393	0.2368411	0.0057471	1
Proportion white	102	0.036181	0.1496807	0	0.9404537
Proportion colored	102	0.0538794	0.1605563	0	0.9826432
Proportion Indian/Asian	102	0.7263002	0.3122672	0	0.9885057

Sources: Republic of South Africa, Department of Education (2000); Republic of South Africa, Statistics South Africa (2001).

Note: The proportion of each population group is used in the census subplace where a school is located.

areas, respectively. Schools under the other former departments for the African population are located in predominantly African residential areas.

To disentangle the spatial relationship between school fees and population composition, Figure 3.3A shows kernel regression line linking school fees to the proportion of whites in a given subplace. Given that the movement of the African population to formerly white residential areas was prohibited under the apartheid regime and is still limited today for financial reasons, the proportion of whites in the population tells us whether a particular school is located in a formerly white area.

Interestingly, in Figure 3.3B the distribution falls into two groups (concentrations). Higher school fees are likely to be charged in the areas where the majority population is white.[14] Figure 3.3 (together with Figure 3.2 and Table 3.1) demonstrates not only the systematic segregation policy in the education system under the apartheid regime, but also that location factors and spatial segregation of different socioeconomic groups (correlated with population groups) are important in determining opportunities for quality education in the next generation.

The Effects of Local Characteristics on School Fees

Table 3.2 shows two sets of results, for South Africa as a whole and for its metropolitan areas (Johannesburg, Cape Town, and Durban) where population inflow has been significant since 1994. Each specification includes district fixed effects.

The points observed in the previous section are confirmed, namely that former education departments and the proportion of whites in the population in a given subplace influence the ability to pay for education quality. In addition, the implications listed in "Empirical Framework and Data" are tested here. Income opportunities are measured by average household income, the average years of schooling in the population aged 20–64, and the unemployment rate. To characterize the economic values of residential areas, the distribution of settlement types and population density from the 2001 census are used.

Column 1 lists factors that represent apartheid regime and type of residential area. First, the proportion of Africans and whites in the population has significant negative and positive effects on school fees, respectively. Colored and Indian/Asian cases have been omitted. It is clear that the spatial segregation of population groups significantly affects school fees.

---

[14] In general Africans move into formerly white residential areas, while whites do not move into predominantly African residential areas. There are some exceptions, such as downtown Johannesburg, where the inflow of Africans adversely affected white businesses, causing whites to move to new suburban areas.

Figure 3.3A School fee and proportion of white population: Kernel

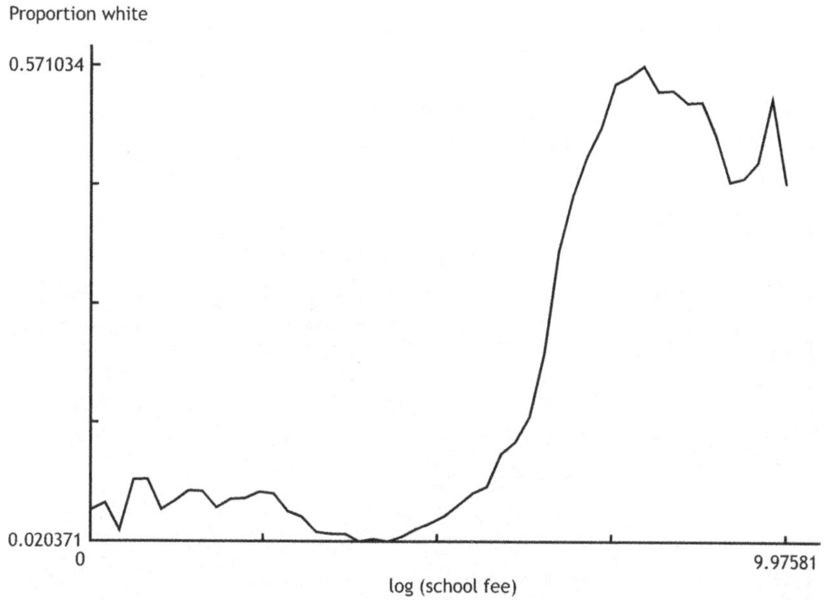

Sources: Republic of South Africa, Department of Education (2000, 2002); Republic of South Africa, Statistics South Africa (2001).

Figure 3.3B School fee and proportion of white population

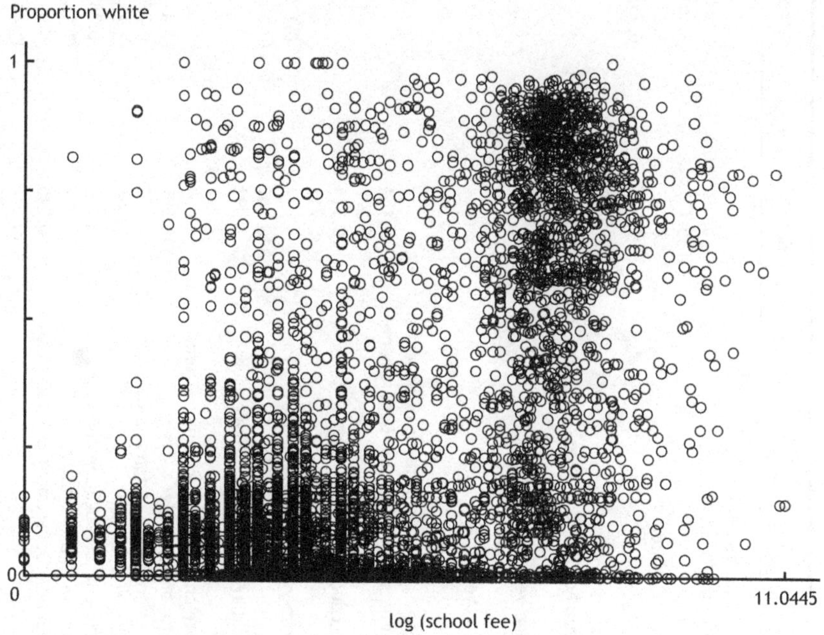

Sources: Republic of South Africa, Department of Education (2000, 2002); Republic of South Africa, Statistics South Africa (2001).

Table 3.2 Determinants of school fees

Sample	South Africa	Metro	South Africa	Metro	South Africa	Metro
Local population group composition						
Proportion African	-0.474	-0.500			-0.412	-0.205
	(5.77)	(3.66)			(4.97)	(1.32)
Proportion white	0.942	1.424			0.674	0.792
	(9.04)	(6.73)			(6.44)	(3.57)
Economic variables						
Ln mean household income			0.171	0.585	0.031	0.213
			(11.25)	(5.19)	(2.71)	(2.47)
Average years of schooling			0.154	0.172	0.071	0.084
			(22.52)	(4.17)	(14.39)	(2.68)
Unemployment rate			-0.140	-2.179	0.008	-0.631
			(2.94)	(5.76)	(0.22)	(2.10)
Former apartheid departments of education						
Bophuthatswana Education Department	0.184				0.060	
	(3.37)				(1.78)	
Ciskei Education Department	0.114				0.073	
	(0.71)				(0.46)	
Department of Education and Training	-0.434	-0.139			-0.419	-0.234
	(10.78)	(0.80)			(10.45)	(1.39)
Gazankulu Department of Education	-0.092				-0.082	
	(1.63)				(1.58)	
Department of Education and Culture:	1.654	1.909			1.662	1.815
House of Assembly	(18.89)	(7.44)			(18.99)	(7.24)
Department of Education and Culture:	0.650	0.777			0.620	0.599
House of Delegates	(7.52)	(3.85)			(7.22)	(3.01)
Department of Education and Culture:	-0.130	0.387			-0.113	0.325
House of Representatives	(1.92)	(1.96)			(1.67)	(1.69)
KwaNdebele Department of Education	-0.040	0.066			-0.069	0.006
	(0.55)	(0.36)			(0.97)	(0.03)
KwaZulu Department of Education	-0.330				-0.331	
	(3.38)				(3.35)	

KaNgwane Department of Education	-0.134	0.156			-0.126	0.107
	(2.97)	(0.79)			(2.80)	(0.56)
Lebowa Department of Education	-0.063	-0.369			-0.074	-0.438
	(1.52)	(1.87)			(1.86)	(2.25)
QwaQwa Department of Education	0.611				0.564	
	(4.58)				(4.20)	
Transvaal Education Department	1.819	2.136			1.865	2.015
	(17.69)	(8.33)			(18.42)	(8.05)
Transkei Education Department	-0.100				-0.087	
	(0.95)				(0.83)	
Venda Education Department	-0.032				-0.050	
	(0.33)				(0.52)	
Location type (%)						
Urban	0.721	0.569	0.901	-0.323	0.535	0.137
	(22.60)	(5.74)	(17.80)	(1.94)	(16.39)	(1.12)
Informal	0.568	0.523	0.738	0.563	0.534	0.447
	(10.73)	(4.79)	(10.71)	(3.39)	(10.69)	(3.75)
Industrial	0.868	0.761	0.570	-0.503	0.758	0.464
	(7.82)	(3.27)	(2.72)	(1.38)	(6.57)	(1.81)
Institutional	0.823	0.902	0.513	0.186	0.520	0.443
	(5.29)	(3.12)	(1.99)	(0.41)	(3.29)	(1.59)
Hostel	0.811	0.248	0.055	-0.481	0.682	0.054
	(5.31)	(0.91)	(0.19)	(0.88)	(4.49)	(0.20)
Population density	-8.31 × 10-06	-0.00002	-0.0001	-0.00002	-9.27 × 10-06	1.01 × 10-06
	(1.72)	(2.01)	(12.94)	(1.77)	(2.02)	(0.13)
R^2	0.6881	0.7939	0.5571	0.6741	0.6934	0.8046
Number of observations	18,564	1,805	18,509	1,804	18,509	1,804

Sources: Republic of South Africa, Department of Education (2000, 2002); Republic of South Africa, Statistics South Africa (2001).

Notes: Dependent variable is log of annual school fee (in rand). Numbers in parentheses are absolute *t*-values, using robust standard errors with census subplace clusters. All specifications include district fixed effects and school type dummies (primary and secondary; combined as the omitted case). For former education departments, schools established since 1994 under the new education department are omitted as the benchmark case (new education department). South Africa and Metro stand for the whole country and the metropolitan areas of Johannesburg, Cape Town, and Durban, respectively.

Second, schools formerly under HOA, HOD, and TED charge significantly higher school fees. The omitted case here is schools established after 1994 under the New Education Department. Combined with previous segregation in residential locations, apartheid still influences school quality.

Third, the distribution of residents among urban, informal, industrial, institutional, or hostel significantly affects school fees. Omitted cases include sparse, tribal, farm, or smallholding settlements. Therefore, schools in urban areas are likely to charge higher school fees, leading to higher education quality. The effect of population density is, however, insignificant.

Column 2 considers metropolitan areas. Although qualitatively similar results were obtained, the magnitude of the parameter estimates for the proportions of Africans and whites in the population is greater than that for the results in column 1. In this sense, population group compositions at the subplace level seem to be more influential in the large cities. Similarly, the effects of HOA, HOD, and TED are larger than in column 1. Hence, it appears that in general the former apartheid regime affects school fees more significantly in these metropolitan areas than in the rest of the country. Population composition, however, is highly correlated with income and level of education.

Columns 3 and 4 focus on factors that represent income opportunities. These variables are expected to be significant if the credit market is imperfect. In the country as a whole, mean household income and average years of schooling (ages 20-64) significantly increase school fees, while the unemployment rate significantly decreases school fees. These results are consistent with the predictions of the simple model described in the section "Dependence of School Quality on Local Resources."

In column 4 the sample is restricted to Johannesburg, Cape Town, and Durban. Mean household income, average years of schooling, and the unemployment rate significantly affect school fees. The income effect is greater here than that in the country as a whole. Consistent with the previous findings on population composition in metropolitan areas, the income gap correlated with population composition matters more in metropolitan areas than nationally. In contrast, the effects of settlement type become weaker in metropolitan areas.

Finally, columns 5 and 6 include apartheid-regime and income opportunity factors. Column 5 shows that both factors matter significantly. The magnitude of the impact, however, differs between the two. While population group composition remains as influential as in columns 1 and 2, the effects of mean household income, average years of schooling, and the unemployment rate become much smaller than in column 3. That is, even though financial and labor-market constraints under the current regime seem to be significant, historical factors originating under the apartheid system (partly correlated with income opportunities) are more significant in the way they constrain the ability to pay for school quality and the quality of schooling investments in the next generation.

In metropolitan areas (column 6), however, the effect of the proportion of Africans in the population decreases by nearly half (from 0.412 to 0.205) and becomes insignificant, while the effect of average income increases from 0.031 to 0.213 and is thus significant. Socioeconomic factors matter more in these large cities than in the country as a whole.

School Quality, Local Resources, and Government Subsidy

This section summarizes estimation results on school quality determination. School quality is measured by LER and the sensitivity of the number of educators to changes in the number of learners, which I construct from SRN 1996 and 2000. An increase in LER implies a decrease in school quality.[15]

In the education function that I estimate, inputs are (log transformed) school fee and per-learner funding from the government. As discussed in previous sections, the school fee for 1998 is taken from the Annual School Survey for 1999. School funding information comes from the KwaZulu-Natal Department of Education.

Table 3.3 shows our empirical results. Columns 1–3 use school fees in different years. The dependent variables are changes in LER from 1996 to 2000. Former population group, school type, and circuit indicators are controlled. Parameters of interest are school fee and per-learner funding. In those columns, the effects of these revenue conditions are significant and negative. Thus a better school financial situation improves school quality. In a preliminary analysis, the log of the 2000 school fee was included, but its effect on dynamic change in the LER from 1996 to 2000 was insignificant. Column 3 uses per-learner total revenue (excluding government funding), which also has a significant and negative effect on LER.

In columns 4 and 5, I test how school financing can change the number of privately employed educators (nonsubsidized educators), controlling changes in the number of learners. First, an increase in the number of learners increases the number of those educators. Second, the log of the 1998 school

[15] The difficulty in identifying the causality arises from potential endogeneity in the number of learners and unobserved fixed components specific to school and community, which are likely to be correlated with school inputs. For example, Lazear (2001) argues that the effect of LER on learner achievement could be empirically ambiguous because of (often unobserved) heterogeneity in learners' quality, that is, discipline. In his model, the optimal size of a class (that is, LER) increases if learners' discipline improves, since the probability of disruption in a classroom decreases. To avoid such a correlation between LER and unobservables, recent studies use exogenous variations (changes) in LER and class size to identify the effect on learner achievement.

Table 3.3 Learner-educator ratio and government subsidy

	Change in learner-educator ratio, 1996-2000			Change in nonsubsidized educators, 1996-2000		Log per-learner government funding, January-March 2000
Explanatory variable	**(1)**	**(2)**	**(3)**	**(4)**	**(5)**	**(6)**
Log school fee, 1998	-0.4204 (1.76)			0.6870 (8.25)	0.7249 (8.48)	-0.1061 (11.73)
Log school fee, 1999		-0.6994 (2.31)				
Log per-learner total revenue, 1998			-0.5481 (1.91)			
Log per-learner government funding (January 1, 2000-March 31, 2000	-8.2887 (10.22)	-8.2919 (10.35)	-7.8244 (9.52)	-0.3378 (3.92)	-0.3341 (3.68)	
Change in number of learners				0.00035 (2.19)	-0.0034 (1.00)	
Change in number of learners × log fee, 1998					0.0013 (2.75)	
Change in number of learners × log funding, 2000					-0.00048 (0.92)	
Learner-educator ratio, 1996						0.0021 (2.92)
School type fixed effects	Yes	Yes	Yes	Yes	Yes	Yes
Former department fixed effects	Yes	Yes	Yes	Yes	Yes	Yes
Circuit fixed effects	Yes	Yes	Yes	Yes	Yes	Yes
Number of observations	3,933	3,947	3,951	4,011	4,011	3,933
R^2	0.1622	0.1315	0.1588	0.4432	0.4569	0.6085

Sources: KwaZulu-Natal, Department of Education (various years); Republic of South Africa, Department of Education (1996, 2000, 2002); Republic of South Africa, Statistics South Africa (2001).

Notes: The numbers in parentheses are absolute *t*-values based on Huber standard errors with circuit clusters. The sample includes schools with positive numbers of educators and learners in both 1996 and 2000, with classrooms in 1996 as recorded in the School Register of Needs, and funded or aided by the government.

fee increases the number of nonsubsidized educators, while government funding decreases the number. Third, and most interestingly, the interaction term of log school fee and change in the number of learners shows a significant positive effect, which implies that with a higher school fee (that is, a greater ability to pay for schooling in the community), an increase in the number of learners can be accommodated by an increase in privately paid educators. These results are consistent with the prediction that communities that are capable of paying for schooling investments will increase the quality of education for the next generation with their own resources.

In the last column, per-learner funding is regressed on the 1998 school fee and 1996 LER with fixed effects of former population group, school type, and circuit. The estimate shows that in 2000 those schools (and areas) that were initially less well endowed were likely to receive more funding from the government.

Conclusions

Neighborhood factors matter, as agents with similar socioeconomic backgrounds are likely to be clustered in the same space. This happens partly because apartheid created inequality in income opportunities (correlated with population groups) and introduced spatial segregation by population group, and partly because even after the abolition of apartheid, financial constraints remained important in choice of residential location, which in turn determines access to income and educational opportunities.

This chapter examined historical and spatial factors that determine education quality and a community's capacity to finance education in post-apartheid South Africa. Our findings show that both historical and financial constraints matter in terms of access to quality education. First, population group compositions created by apartheid (especially proportions of Africans and whites) at the subplace level and by the former departments of education significantly affect school fees and therefore quality of education. Higher school fees are charged in residential areas with a large proportion of whites in the population. Second, average income, schooling, and unemployment rate at the subplace level also influence the determination of school fees, a finding that implies the existence of an imperfect credit market.

Migration to cities became unrestricted when legal constraints were lifted after the abolishment of apartheid, and thus income mobility is now more dynamic in urban areas. As a result financial constraints are more important and population composition is less important in large cities. Wealthier households can move to well-off (that is, formerly white) residential areas to send their children to better schools, a practice that was formerly prohibited. This is happening in the areas surrounding large cities.

This chapter also demonstrated that government subsidy can improve the quality of schooling, despite the fact that school quality largely depends on local resource availability. Government subsidies, if progressively allocated to lower-quality schools with a poorer resource base, can potentially disconnect the linkage between local resources and school quality. To narrow the current imbalance, the government should increase financial and personnel support to disadvantaged locales and schools by targeting specific areas—as its progressive subsidy allocation has recently begun to do.

If this direct option is limited owing to government budget constraints, alternative strategies may require the redistribution of fees from richer to poorer schools or the implementation of programs that more explicitly move certain kinds of children to better schools—including busing and school vouchers—as already adopted in developed countries.

In this chapter I did not account for more qualitative factors, such as the quality of teachers and school management. It is puzzling why learner achievement in South Africa still differs so widely across population groups despite the equalization (albeit very gradual) of school inputs, such as those measured by LER. There is a need to pay equal or even greater attention to qualitative inputs within the school system, in addition to the highly progressive subsidy allocations.

PART 2

Household Behavior

Part 2 examines household behavior in human capital formation using micro panel data. Chapter 4 analyzes the formation of human capital from early-childhood nutrition intake to schooling investments and outcomes. Chapter 5 examines adolescents' transition from school to the labor market, with a particular focus on the effect of prime-age adult mortality shocks on their behavior. This chapter also provides evidence of increased prime-age mortality, which implies that the expected returns to human capital investments are being altered in South Africa.

CHAPTER 4

Early-Childhood Nutrition, Schooling, and Sibling Inequality

Human capital takes a long time to accumulate; it passes through several phases from early childhood through higher education. While nutritional intake in early childhood forms the basis for a child's health capital, which in turn provides a foundation for subsequent child development, investments in schooling augment the child's knowledge capital, which is directly rewarded in advanced labor markets and in dealing with advanced production technologies.[1] In this chapter I examine the effects of nutritional status and health capital in early childhood on schooling investments and outcomes, using recently available panel data from South Africa.

The dynamic process of human capital development creates the possibility that investments in early childhood will influence the optimal amount and effectiveness of investments at later stages (Cunha et al. 2004). Several studies have attempted to identify the link between early-childhood nutritional status and schooling outcomes (for example, Glewwe, Jacoby, and King 2001; Alderman, Hoddinott, and Kinsey 2006) and adult outcomes (for example, Smith 2005; Behrman et al. 2006; Maluccio et al. 2009).[2] In general, the way in which early-stage human capital investments determine the subsequent path of human capital accumulation and future income depends on (1) whether investments in different stages are mutual complements or substitutes and (2) the extent to which early investments and outcomes alter the environment, information, and preferences of children and parents in ways that affect investment decisions at later stages.

To answer the question of whether early investments in children affect future outcomes requires an understanding of the complex interactions of market forces and household behavior. First, there is an input-output relationship

[1] For comprehensive discussions of the problem of child malnutrition in economic development, see Behrman, Alderman, and Hoddinott (2004).

[2] Black, Devereux, and Salvanes (2007) also found significant effects of birth weight on adult outcomes.

between health and schooling in the human capital production function. For example, if health capital is an input in the schooling production function, enabling children to attend classes every day, whether health capital augments the productivity of schooling investments or substitutes for schooling inputs, it affects the optimal level of schooling investments.[3] In the former case, I predict a cumulative process of widening inequality among siblings, given differences in nutritional status and health capital in early childhood, since healthy children tend to have better schooling outcomes. If parents are averse to sibling inequality in future earnings, however, they will make greater schooling investments in unhealthy children.

Second, parents learn about potential returns to schooling investments from the outcomes of early-stage investments (in nutritional status and health, in our context) and make decisions regarding optimal investments at later stages. In these decisions, parents' preferences concerning sibling inequality in human capital and future income matter. If parents are averse to inequality among their children, they may increase investments in the schooling of their less well-endowed children to equalize the children's future incomes (Quisumbing, Estudillo, and Otsuka 2003). In the context of human capital production, since the outcomes of early-childhood investments signal the expected outcomes of investment at a later stage, parents can react to those signals by changing late-stage investments to maximize their objectives.

Third, health capital, as well as schooling investments, generates positive economic returns, especially in the developing-country context (Strauss 1986; Haddad and Bouis 1991; Thomas and Strauss 1997). Therefore, health capital may increase opportunity costs for schooling investments (that is, higher wages), and it may affect intertemporal decisionmaking, creating heterogeneity in the effect of health capital on schooling investments.

In empirically assessing this issue, we encounter challenging problems even with longitudinal data for children. The first problem arises from the potential endogeneity of nutritional status; fixed household-specific unobserved factors may affect both child health capital and schooling decisions, creating a positive correlation between them. To eliminate this problem, our approach requires household fixed effects, which base inference on (often small) sibling variations.[4]

---

[3] Health capital is a part of human capital, measuring physical development and conditions in children (height, weight, and health status) but not including such endowments as inborn differences in intelligence.

[4] The literature offers a few qualified empirical studies, which solve these problems. Employing longitudinal data for children from Zimbabwe, Alderman, Hoddinott, and Kinsey (2006) use civil war and drought periods that affected growth in children below the age of 3 to identify the effect of early-childhood malnutrition on schooling in a maternal fixed-effect model. This iden-

The next section describes the model. Human capital accumulation is modeled as a sequential process in which health is formed at an early stage and schooling investment is undertaken depending on health outcomes. Both health and knowledge (education) capital determine earnings in the labor market. The section on data discusses econometric issues, focusing on specification and identification strategy.

Data and variables are described in the section "Outcomes at the Early Stage of Schooling." To measure schooling outcomes, I use the 2004 KwaZulu-Natal Income Dynamics Study (round 3), which collected individual-level information such as enrollment, age schooling started, grade completed, grades repeated, and expenditures from children aged 7–20.[5] To supplement the main analysis, the survey also used the results of simple mathematics tests given to children aged 7–9 to measure their learning performance. Therefore, combined with the information on nutrition and health outcomes for children aged 1–5 available in the 1998 survey, I can investigate the effect of early-childhood nutrition on schooling investments and outcomes of children aged 6 years and above. One advantage of focusing on the early stages of schooling is the high enrollment rate at the primary school level, which minimizes a selectivity problem arising from time allocation decisions for children at later stages of schooling.

The section "Outcomes at the Later Stage of Schooling" summarizes empirical results. First, data for siblings showing the effects of nutrition (as indicated by height) on the age schooling started and the grade completed demonstrate that for the majority, children of normal height (as measured by

---

tification strategy is based on findings that under credit-constrained circumstances, income shocks (such as drought and flood) change consumption, which affects child growth (Foster 1995; Hoddinott and Kinsey 2001). Glewwe, Jacoby, and King (2001) take a similar approach to sibling estimation, using longitudinal data on Filipino children, but their identification strategy uses information on older siblings when the child was younger than 3 years. Alderman et al. (2000) use price data, interacted with parents' education and child gender, as an instrument for child height growth in Pakistan. This chapter uses information on the availability of healthcare personnel in sample communities in 1993, right before most children in the 1998 sample were born. During South Africa's transition to a democratic nation, the government implemented pro-poor interventions in the health sector by building healthcare facilities and increasing the numbers of healthcare personnel. Our identification strategy uses these post-apartheid dynamics, captured by age (birth year), which differ across differently endowed communities.

[5] The survey is representative in the province of KwaZulu-Natal, which has the largest population in the country. We do not have any reason for attributing our findings specifically to education systems in the province and the Zulu families in particular. For political reasons, however, this province experienced more violent turmoil than other provinces during the transition from apartheid to democracy, which delayed the implementation of the first national democratic election to 1995. This situation might have more adversely affected schooling behavior among children who entered school during the transition period in KwaZulu-Natal than in other provinces.

height-for-age z-score) start school earlier, complete more grades, and repeat fewer grades. The analysis also identifies some outlying observations among taller children (who make up less than 5 percent of the sample) that show a negative effect of the height z-score on schooling outcomes. However, it also remains highly possible that ages for these children in 1998 were underreported, so their height z-scores were overestimated. I also find that, although better nutrition and health status in early childhood improve primary school outcomes, this positive effect diminishes over time as children age. The smaller effect observed among older siblings may also reflect the fact that the effect of nutrition on height is large among children aged less than 3 (in 1998), and height may rebound afterward.[6]

Second, the analysis of mathematics test results, using the sample of children aged 7-9, shows that health capital, measured by height in early childhood, has a significantly positive effect, implying that early-childhood nutrition affects learning performance at the early stage of transition to schooling.

Empirical Strategy

This section describes the empirical framework used to assess the effects of early-childhood health capital on schooling decisions and outcomes at a subsequent stage. The schooling equation is

$$q_{ijt} = \alpha + \beta^1 h_{ijt-1} \sum_H \beta^1_H h_{ijt-1} I(h_{ijt-1} \in H) + \sum_a \beta^1_a h_{ijt-1} I(a_{ijt} = a) +$$
$$\sum_a \beta^2_a I(a_{ijt} = a) + x_{ijt}\gamma + \mu_i + \phi_j + \nu_{ijt},$$

where i, j, and t denote household, child, and time, respectively, and q_{ijt} is schooling inputs or outcomes; h_{ijt-1} is health capital, which is measured by the height-for-age z-score (formed at $t - 1$); a_{ijt} is the age of the child; x_{ijt} is a set of control variables; μ_i is a household-specific fixed effect; ϕ_j is child-specific fixed unobservables; and ν_{ijt} is an error term.

First, it is important to control the heterogeneity that arises from the current ages. For example, cumulative years of grades repeated increases (but weakly) as children spend more time in school, that is, as their age increases. The score on the numerical tests also changes by age (and grade completed). In the analysis that follows, I assume that age structure in the sample of chil-

[6] Children aged 0-5 in the 1993 sample entered school during the transition period 1993-98, while children aged 1-5 in the 1998 sample entered school during the more stable period 1998-2004. This latter period was after basic school reforms had been introduced—that is, the South African School Act in 1996 and the National Norms and Standards for School Funding in 1998—though their implementation took longer. This change might have affected child schooling behavior and parents' decisions.

dren is exogenous; it is uncorrelated with shocks in schooling decisions and outcomes, an assumption which justifies the inclusion of age fixed effects.[7]

Second, since it is highly likely that household-specific unobservables μ_i are correlated with h_{ijt-1}, OLS estimates of β_1 are biased. This makes it necessary to eliminate this component from the errors. For this purpose, I include household fixed effects to control μ_i. Therefore, the estimation is based on variations across siblings in the household (that is, within-sibling estimates).

In the context of panel analysis, the inclusion of household fixed effects has another advantage regarding the attrition bias. Since we look only at within-household variations, given household observations in the two rounds, we do not have to control for household-level attrition problems. Individual-level attritions are investigated in the section "Data Sources" (see Table 4.3).

With household fixed effects, however, we use only within-household variations from the sample of multiple-child households. Dropping observations from single-child households reduces the size of our sample, which potentially decreases the precision of parameter estimates in our analysis.

Third, even with household fixed effects, we still encounter a potential problem of bias that may arise from a correlation between ϕ_j and h_{ijt}. To eliminate this correlation, it is necessary to use a set of instruments that explains the variations in h_{ijt-1} but is uncorrelated with either ϕ_j or shocks in schooling investments and outcomes ε_{ijt}. However, the necessity depends on the magnitude of covariations in differences among siblings in the z-score and schooling endowments.

For this purpose, we use the information on whether each community (cluster) had different types of healthcare personnel—doctor, nurse, pharmacist, trained midwife, family planning worker, community healthcare worker, or traditional birth attendant—in t - 2 (1993 in our setting), interacted by child age.[8] The 1993 initial condition of healthcare personnel availability should

---

[7] Since we only use preschool children in the sample, we can exclude the possibility that parents observe the schooling outcomes of older children before making reproductive (childbirth) decisions. However, as discussed, it is still possible that the health outcomes of older children in the preschool period affect reproductive decisions.

[8] The data include information on the distance from the community to the nearest personnel if the community has no personnel. The data also have information on types of healthcare facilities in the community, number of healthcare facilities, and if they do not exist, distance to the nearest one. In this chapter, however, we use only the indicator of whether communities had those personnel.

In an early version, an instrument was constructed as follows. First, define the indicator, which has the value of one if children were less than 3 years old (inclusive) between the beginning of 1994 and the end of 1995. The period before the age of 3 is regarded as that when a child's growth is most sensitive to nutritional intake, which reflects economic conditions. This indicator is interacted with cluster fixed effects to capture possible heterogeneity in the impacts of the 1994–95 disturbances on child growth, I(Age 3 in year = 1994 or 1995) × cluster have affected subsequent changes in the numbers of community-level healthcare personnel after 1994, given the fact that South Africa has attempted to build healthcare facilities and increase the number of healthcare personnel in the post-apartheid period. However, it is hard to show quantitative evidence for this conjecture from our sample.

In the following estimation, I interact child age with the initial number of healthcare personnel to capture dynamic changes in the personnel specific to a given community. For example, if a nurse was not in the community in 1993, it is likely that the community would have nurses in the subsequent period. Therefore, the interaction between the initial availability of healthcare personnel and child age (cohort) captures community-specific changes in healthcare conditions.[9] Another advantage of interacting the healthcare information with child age comes from the fact that nutrition input is most important in children under 3 years of age, an outcome measured by height in our context. The impact of healthcare on height differs by child age. The individual-level variations, created by age, make it feasible to examine intrahousehold (within-sibling) variations in health and schooling outcomes in the household fixed-effect model.

However, we also notice a possibility that dynamic changes in healthcare and education facilities are correlated, though both sets of changes were slow to occur at the beginning of the post-apartheid government. In the first stage, we are concerned with the impact of potential changes in health infrastructure on the health outcomes of the sample children during the period 1993-98, while their schooling outcomes were directly affected by changes in education infrastructure in 1998-2004. This time gap may justify the use of the 1993 initial health infrastructure data (personnel availability) as a potential source of intercommunity variations. However, to the extent that (changes in) healthcare facilities and schools are correlated, the proposed instrument is invalid.

---

indicators. This period also corresponds to the abolishment of apartheid, so new economic opportunities were presented to the African population. On the other hand, unrest associated with the transition was particularly violent in the province of KwaZulu-Natal. Thus there could have been positive impacts as well as negative ones. In addition, to capture the heterogeneity in the impacts related to the initial income level, the indicator is also interacted with total monthly household income in 1993. Although an *F*-test supports the joint significance of these instruments in explaining variations among siblings in height-for-age z-scores, a Hausman-Wu test rejects the relevance of these instruments. We observed some differences between within-sibling OLS and within-sibling instrumental-variable estimates, but the magnitude did not alter the qualitative nature of our results.

[9] Age distribution is potentially endogenous, correlated with private information on policy changes that parents might have had when the society moved into the post-apartheid regime. Parents might have changed reproductive behavior and their fertility might have changed; these factors affect birth timing and therefore the initial health conditions for their children.

In the analysis, I use the information on nurses, community healthcare workers, and traditional birth attendants since a preliminary examination suggested that they are particularly important (that is, statistically significant). Since I also include age fixed effects when estimating schooling equations in the household fixed-effect model, the average cohort effects are controlled.

I also use the weight-for-age z-score as an instrument to eliminate measurement errors in the height z-score. Results will be compared between the two different sets of instruments.

The first-stage regression results are shown in Table 4.1, where the identifying instruments are jointly significant. Interestingly, the result (controlling for age fixed effects) implies that in communities with some nurses in 1993, younger children (those who were born more recently) have gained height relative to older children. On the other hand, older children have gained height (relative to younger children) in communities which had community healthcare workers and traditional birth attendants in 1993. The difference may imply some endogeneity of the initial allocation of healthcare personnel. However, the fact that I examine intrahousehold variations in child health outcome makes this issue less problematic. On the other hand, the weight-for-age z-score has a significant positive effect on the height-for-age z-score.

Data Sources

The analysis requires information from different points in time for the same individuals. In this chapter, I use data from the KIDS of 1993, 1998, and 2004 (see Chapter 1). The sample was population self-weighted in the first round in 1993, based on the 1991 population census, and enumeration-based weights were introduced in 1998. The 1993 and 1998 surveys provide information on anthropometric measures and health outcomes of children, enabling us to construct age-standardized z-scores for height. The 2004 survey provides some detailed information on schooling decisions and outcomes. Our analysis combines the nutritional status of pre-primary-school-age children in 1998 and 1993 and their schooling inputs and outcomes until 2004.[10]

In the principal analysis, I use as schooling variables (1) age schooling started, (2) grade completed (conditional on current age), (3) number of grades repeated, and (4) mathematics test results. For age schooling started, the 2004 survey asks for the calendar year in which the child started primary school.

[10] Constructing individual-level panel data from the 1998 and 2004 surveys, we have screened out observations recorded in multiple households (multiple memberships). The details of this procedure are available from the author.

Table 4.1 Height-for-age z-score

Explanatory variable	(1)	(2)
Nurse × age	-0.2921	
	(1.54)	
Community health worker × age	0.8950	
	(2.84)	
Traditional birth attendant × age	0.2360	
	(1.70)	
Weight-for-age z-score		0.3546
		(2.59)
Age 8 years	0.2434	0.4288
	(0.54)	(0.96)
Age 9 years	-1.9111	-0.6920
	(2.56)	(1.64)
Age 10 years	-0.8080	-0.3939
	(1.67)	(0.95)
Age 11 years	-0.1691	0.2061
	(0.30)	(0.39)
Female	0.1526	0.0114
	(0.52)	(0.04)
Household fixed effects	Yes	Yes
F-statistic (all variables)	2.88	3.15
(*p*-value)	(0.0062)	(0.0071)
F-statistic (identifying instrumental variable)	3.55	*t*-value above
(*p*-value)	(0.0171)	
Within-household R^2	0.1828	0.1524
Number of children	199	199
Number of households	88	88

Sources: South African Labour and Development Research Unit, University of Cape Town (1994); University of KwaZulu-Natal / International Food Policy Research Institute / University of Wisconsin-Madison (1998, 2004).

Notes: The dependent variable is height-for-age z-score. Numbers in parentheses are absolute *t*-values. Estimation with household fixed effects uses children from households with multiple siblings. Specification includes over-age and under-age indicators for reported age in 1998. Sample consists of children aged 1-5 years in 1998, with consistent ages between 1998 and 2004, and height-for-age z-score in the range -6 to 6 in 1993. Age 7 years is omitted.

That year, compared with the current age in 2004, tells us the age at which the child started attending primary school.[11]

Table 4.2 reports the descriptive statistics of schooling outcome variables: age started school, the highest grade completed, and the cumulative number of grades repeated. First, the age started school increases as the current age

[11] In the principal analysis, we use only observations for which the estimated age schooling started was greater or equal to 4 years, restricting the sample to children who were aged less than 4 years.

Table 4.2 Descriptive statistics: Schooling

Age (years)	Age started school	Grades completed	Grades repeated
6	5.288	0.714	0.143
	(0.756)	(0.756)	(0.378)
7	5.693	0.894	0.256
	(0.922)	(0.689)	(0.597)
8	5.921	1.597	0.366
	(0.829)	(0.764)	(0.540)
9	6.150	2.443	0.343
	(0.989)	(1.049)	(0.563)
10	6.171	3.216	0.552
	(1.064)	(1.168)	(0.777)
11	6.048	4.123	0.628
	(1.434)	(1.398)	(0.876)
12	6.216	5.121	0.609
	(1.470)	(1.469)	(0.897)
13	6.220	6.038	0.616
	(1.281)	(1.480)	(0.946)
14	6.431	6.869	0.711
	(1.322)	(1.468)	(0.968)
15	6.485	7.559	0.925
	(1.282)	(1.445)	(1.047)
16	6.406	8.534	0.776
	(1.399)	(1.855)	(1.016)
17	6.516	9.036	1.195
	(1.511)	(1.790)	(1.241)
18	6.665	9.604	1.227
	(1.951)	(2.052)	(1.223)
19	7.189	9.875	1.263
	(1.772)	(1.815)	(1.186)
20	7.390	9.889	1.188
	(2.140)	(2.539)	(1.106)

Source: University of KwaZulu-Natal (2004).
Notes: Means are shown with standard deviations in parentheses. There are seven observations in the age 6 years group, though the Children Module of Section 12 targets children aged 7–20 years.

increases, which suggests that younger cohorts enter school at an earlier age. Second, the highest grade completed and the cumulative number of grades repeated also increase with the current age.

In the mathematical tests, the team implemented four types of numerical tests for children aged 7–9: addition, subtraction, multiplication, and division. The four questions were 3 + 5 (addition), 7 – 3 (subtraction), 2 × 6 (multiplication), and 12 ÷ 4 (division). Table 4.3 reports the number of observations with correct and incorrect answers. Note that the sample size for each age group is nearly the same. First, the likelihood of giving a correct answer increases as age increases for all four questions. Second, the difficulty increases as we move from addition to division.

Table 4.3 Descriptive statistics: Mathematical test results

	Age (years)		
Test	7	8	9
Addition			
Correct	157	186	189
Incorrect	61	27	16
Subtraction			
Correct	117	157	166
Incorrect	101	56	39
Multiplication			
Correct	60	98	131
Incorrect	158	115	74
Division			
Correct	15	44	77
Incorrect	203	169	128
Number of observations	218	213	205

Source: University of KwaZulu-Natal (2004).

Table 4.4 reports the determinants of attrition from the 1998 to the 2004 round and from the 1993 to the 2004 round (see Fitzgerald, Gottschalk, and Moffitt 1998a, 1998b; Thomas, Frankenberg, and Smith 2001). Since our principal analysis focuses on variations among siblings, controlling for household fixed effects, attritions at the individual level are of interest. Given observations in the 1998 round, our concern here is to determine whether the probability of being observed in the 2004 round depends on explanatory variables used in the schooling investment and outcome equations. The sample is restricted to children from households found in 2004 who were between the ages of 1 and 5 in 1998 (0–5 in 1993) with height-for-age *z*-score values between -6 and 6.

In the attrition analysis, I use explanatory variables from the schooling equations: the height-for-age z-score, age indicators, and gender dummy, which are taken from either the 1993 or the 1998 round. To the extent that these predetermined variables are not correlated with attrition, we would not expect bias in estimates in the schooling equations owing to the attrition process. However, a possibility of attrition on unobservables still remains. For example, because of a correlation between shocks (unobservables) in the attrition and schooling equations, attrition on unobservables may cause additional bias in the schooling equations.[12]

[12] Fitzgerald, Gottschalk, and Moffit (1998a, 1998b) discuss the issues of attrition on observables and unobservables and examine attrition problems in the Panel Study of Income Dynamics.

Table 4.4 Attritions

	Percentage attrition				
	1998-2004			1993-2004	
Explanatory variable	**(1)**	**(2)**	**(3)**	**(4)**	**(5)**
Height-for-age z-score		0.0081	0.0045		0.0126
		(0.62)	(0.31)		(0.83)
Age 0 (less than 1 year old)				21.50	
Age 1 year	13.27			24.39	-0.0256
					(0.34)
Age 2 years	11.11	0.0750	0.1585	19.70	0.0145
		(1.27)	(2.35)		(0.20)
Age 3 years	5.60	0.0632	0.1125	20.30	-0.0425
		(1.10)	(1.76)		(0.60)
Age 4 years	6.38	0.0636	0.0940	26.13	-0.0840
		(1.08)	(1.40)		(1.12)
Age 5 years	4.69	0.1176	0.1588	12.90	0.0082
		(1.88)	(2.29)		(0.11)
Female	7.84	-0.0503	-0.1069	18.03	0.0329
		(1.24)	(2.29)		(0.76)
Male	9.39			24.25	
			Household fixed effects		
		1998	2004		1998
Number of children		513	513		689
Number of attritions		44	44		145
Number of children in estimation		304	252		456
Number of households with multiple siblings		121	108		181
Adjusted R^2 (with household dummies)		0.1132	0.1121		0.2266
Within-household R^2		0.0291	0.0780		0.0145

Sources: South African Labour and Development Research Unit, University of Cape Town (1994); University of KwaZulu-Natal / International Food Policy Research Institute / University of Wisconsin-Madison (1998, 2004).

Notes: Dependent variable equals one if observed in 2004 and zero otherwise. Estimation uses the linear probability model. Numbers in parentheses are absolute *t*-values. Sample consists of children with height-for-age z-scores between -6 and 6 from households observed in both 1993 or 1998 and 2004. Estimation uses children from households with multiple siblings. There were 44 attritions out of 513 children and 145 attritions out of 689 children in the periods 1998-2004 and 1993-2004, respectively. Age is defined as years old in the initial year, 1998 for columns 1-3 and 1993 for columns 4 and 5, respectively.

Specifications include household fixed effects with initial age and gender indicators. Column 1 shows the 1998-2004 attrition rates by age and gender group. Attrition probability decreases as children age, which suggests a high mortality rate in early childhood; mobility of very young children as mothers, families, and households devise ways of providing childcare; or both. Columns 2 and 3 use household fixed effects based on the 1998 and 2004 households, respectively. During the six-year interval between the two rounds, households were split and young people formed new households. The analysis in the next section uses the 2004 household definition, since decisions regarding child schooling are supposed to be made in current household units.[13] In both cases, age in 1998 affects the likelihood of being observed in 2004. This suggests that child mortality and mobility depend on the age of the child.

Column 4 shows the 1993-2004 attrition rates. Age-specific attrition rates are higher than those in the 1998–2004 case, because we cover a longer period. We do not observe a clear relationship between attrition rate and initial age. In both cases, boys show a higher attrition rate than girls. Column 5 reports determinants of attrition from 1993 to 2004. Contrary to the 1998-2004 case, initial age is not significant.

In the analysis of nutrition-height effects on schooling, we screen out observations of children that show ages inconsistent with the 2004 round. For example, age 8 in 2004 corresponds to age 1, 2, or 3 in 1998. Discrepancies arise from the timing of the surveys and birthdays.[14] Mostly for this reason, sample size differs between the attrition analysis and the schooling analysis. Screening out observations of inconsistent ages between 1998 and 2004 with reference to ages reported in the 2004 survey, in particular, excludes large height-for-age z-scores as a result of understated ages in 1998.[15] The same procedure is applied to age matching between 1993 and 2004. In the analysis of schooling outcomes, I include over-age and under-age indicators to control for the birthday effect, in addition to age fixed effects.

In fixed-effect models, I use only observations of children from fixed-effect units with multiple children. For example, with household fixed effects, I use households with multiple siblings. This procedure excludes spurious observations from the estimation process.

Outcomes at the Early Stage of Schooling

Age Schooling Started

Table 4.5 shows the effect of the height-for-age z-score in 1998 on the age at which school was started. The sample consists of children aged 1–4 in 1998

---

[13] Preliminary analysis shows that there are no significant differences even if we use the 1998 units.

[14] The 1998 survey asked for "approximate" current age, wording that I believe caused variations in reported age.

[15] We find some negative effects of large height-for-age z-scores on schooling outcomes. One possibility is that ages were underreported in a previous round, a situation that causes overestimation of height-for-age z-scores for those children. However, by screening out observations with ages inconsistent between rounds, this possibility can be minimized.

Table 4.5 Age at which school was started

Explanatory variable	(1)	(2)	(3)	(4)
Height-for-age z-score, 1998	-0.0827	-0.1367	-0.4790	-0.1477
	(2.87)	(1.78)	(1.98)	(1.10)
Female	-0.0474	-0.1766	-0.2957	-0.1805
	(0.47)	(0.98)	(1.28)	(0.98)
Current age fixed effects	Yes	Yes	Yes	Yes
Cluster fixed effects	Yes			
Household fixed effects		Yes	Yes	Yes
Sargan overidentification (*p*-value)			13.052	n.a.
			(0.0015)	
Mean age started	6.0155	6.1717	6.1717	6.1717
Mean height-for-age z-score	-0.7164	-0.6892	-0.6892	-0.6892
Within-cluster R^2	0.1763			
Within-household R^2		0.4541	0.2138	0.4539
Number of children	322	99	99	99
Number of groups	55	46	46	46

Sources: South African Labour and Development Research Unit, University of Cape Town (1994); University of KwaZulu-Natal / International Food Policy Research Institute / University of Wisconsin-Madison (1998, 2004).

Notes: Dependent variable is age at which school was started. Numbers in parentheses are absolute *t*-values. Estimation with household (cluster) fixed effects uses children from households (clusters) with multiple children. Specifications include age fixed effects, and over-age and under-age indicators for reported age in 1998. Sample consists of children aged 1-4 years in 1998 and 7 years or above in 2004, with consistent ages between 1998 and 2004, height-for-age z-score in the range -6 to 6 in 1998, and age at which school was started equal to 4 years or above. In column 4, the equation is just identified. n.a. means not available.

and aged 7 or above in 2004.[16] Column 1 controls only cluster-level fixed effects, while Columns 2 and 3 report within-sibling estimates. The specifications include current age indicators to control cohort effects. In column 1, greater child height is found to significantly lower the age at which the child started school, though this estimate is likely to be biased owing to a correlation between household-level factors and child height.

[16] Since older children are more likely to be already in school than younger children, this type of sample selection affects estimated height effects on age schooling started. If the height effect is positive, those who are relatively well endowed are likely to be dropped from the sample, especially among older children (ages 4 and 5). As a result, the selection biases the estimate upward (smaller in absolute value).

The enrollment rates among children age 7 or above are quite high in this sample (KIDS round 3, Section 12.2): 99.04 percent (age 7), 100 percent (age 8), 99.51 percent (age 9), 99.51 percent (age 10), and 98.73 percent (age 11). Therefore, omitting children who had not started schooling is not consequential.

Column 2 confirms this finding, showing an even greater effect of height on age schooling started. The upward bias suggests that household-specific endowment (which increases the child's age) is positively correlated with the height-for-age z-score. Column 3 shows the instrumental variables estimation result, which implies upward bias owing to the correlation between individual-level endowment and the height-for-age z-score. It is also likely that the difference between columns 2 and 3 might have captured measurement errors in the reported age schooling started. The marginal impact of the height-for-age z-score on the age schooling started is even larger in column 3. To eliminate measurement errors, the weight-for-age z-score is used as an instrument in column 4. The parameter estimate is comparable to that in column 2, which suggests that measurement errors are not a large issue here. These results imply that early-childhood malnutrition delays the age at which a child starts school.[17]

Current age does not influence age schooling started (not shown in the table), which suggests that the decision to start primary schooling did not change between 1998 and 2004.[18] Thus there is no systematic change in the behavior of entering school across cohorts during the period.

Grade Completed

Table 4.6 reports the effects of the height-for-age z-score on years of schooling. As children have not completed schooling, specifications include age dummies which standardize years of schooling. Columns 1 and 2 compare estimates with cluster and household fixed effects. Though a positive significant effect is found with cluster fixed effects, the effect is negative and insignificant with household fixed effects. In both cases, girls are more likely to advance grades than boys.

To see slope differences, column 3 interacts the height-for-age z-score with an indicator which takes the value of one if the height-for-age z-score is above 2 and zero otherwise. In this case, an improvement in the height-for-age z-score increases years of schooling completed, but the slope turns out to be negative at large values of the z-score (2–6). In column 4, I also include age

---

[17] A preliminary analysis showed some potential nonmonotonicity in the effect of the height-for-age z-score on the age schooling started. First, estimates of height effects on the age schooling started are significantly negative among relatively short children. Marginal gain (earlier age) from increasing height is greater among less well-endowed children. Second, the number of observations in these estimations suggests that the effect is negative and significant in more than 95 percent of the sample. Some outlying observations from exceptionally tall children (conditional on age) change the estimates. This also holds in the analysis of grade completion and repetitions.

[18] There was no change in the official starting age.

Table 4.6 Grade completed

Explanatory variable	(1)	(2)	(3)	(4)	(5)	(6)	(7)
Haz	0.0510	-0.0670	0.1074	0.4001	0.0721	0.5092	0.3117
	(1.93)	(1.18)	(1.41)	(3.18)	(0.86)	(1.59)	(1.20)
Haz × I (Haz 2-6 years)			-0.4101	-0.6167			
			(3.21)	(4.26)			
Haz × age 8 years				-0.1643			
				(1.16)			
Haz × age 9 years				-0.5689			
				(3.02)			
Haz × age 10 years				-0.3936			
				(2.59)			
Haz × age 11 years				-0.3319			
				(1.78)			
Female	0.1918	0.5928	0.6202	0.5791	0.5987	0.6906	0.6491
	(2.08)	(3.34)	(3.70)	(3.40)	(3.27)	(3.02)	(3.22)
Current age fixed effects	Yes	Yes	Yes	Yes	Yes	Yes	Yes
Cluster fixed effects	Yes						
Household fixed effects		Yes	Yes	Yes	Yes	Yes	Yes
Sargan overidentification (*p*-value)						2.081	n.a.
						(0.3534)	
Mean grade completed	2.1850	2.0774	2.0774	2.0774	2.0078	2.0078	2.0078
Mean Haz	-0.7128	-0.5106	-0.5106	-0.5106	-0.9245	-0.9245	-0.9245
Within-cluster R^2	0.5628	0.7038	0.7395	0.7737	0.7056	0.5759	0.6667
Number of children	400	155	155	155	128	128	128
Number of groups	60	71	71	71	58	58	58

Sources: South African Labour and Development Research Unit, University of Cape Town (1994); University of KwaZulu-Natal / International Food Policy Research Institute / University of Wisconsin-Madison (1998, 2004).

Notes: Dependent variable is grade completed. Numbers in parentheses are absolute *t*-values. Estimation with household (cluster) fixed effects uses children from households (clusters) with multiple children. Specifications include age fixed effects, and over-age and under-age indicators for reported age in 1998. Sample consists of children aged 1-4 years in 1998, with consistent ages between 1998 and 2004 and height-for-age *z*-score in the range -6 to 6 in 1998 (columns 5-7: -6 to 2 in 1998). In column 7 the equation is just identified. Haz means height-for-age z-score, 1998; I means indicator function; n.a. means not available.

interactions to investigate how the height effect changes as the child ages. The height-for-age z-score improves schooling while the effect becomes negative when the score is large. We also find that the effect diminishes as the child ages, particularly after age 9.

To interpret these findings, we must take into account two possibilities. First, if age was underreported in 1998 for some reason, the expected years of schooling completed in 2004 would be smaller, which makes it more likely to find a negative estimate of the height effect among those large children. Second, we cannot deny the possibility that large children have a high opportunity cost of schooling as returns to their health capital are positive in the labor market or, more generally, in nonschool activities (though this point is not proven in this chapter). Note that the opportunity costs for those healthy children do not arise solely from strictly defined labor market activities, but also from nonschool activities, including informal work (usually not captured in statistics), household work, and crime.

The concavity found previously also suggests that parents are averse to inequality among siblings. Given that healthy (taller) children earn more in the labor market, parents may invest more in less healthy (shorter) children to decrease the inequality in human capital and future earnings. Recall that the aversion to inequality may be traced to the concavity of the parents' utility function.

The observation that the height effect diminishes as the child ages suggests another possibility. If it is height-for-age before age 3 which matters most and height may also rebound afterward, height at an older age (still ≤ 5 years) explains fewer of the latter outcomes than height at earlier ages. Alternatively, if returns to height (health capital) increase as the child ages, the incentive to work (to study) increases (decreases).

In columns 5–7, I compare within-sibling and within-sibling instrumental-variable estimates using the sample of children with z-scores below 2. Column 6 uses as instruments the initial availability of healthcare personnel interacted with age, whereas column 7 uses the weight-for-age z-score. It is found in columns 5 and 6 that the instrumental-variable estimate for the height-for-age z-score effect is greater than the within-sibling effect, which suggests downward bias. Higher endowment in academic performance is negatively correlated with early-childhood health capital.[19] Though the difference might have captured measurement errors in reported grades completed, this possibility is less likely than in the case of age schooling started.

[19] Our result shows that higher health endowment discourages academic advancement, probably because there is another incentive for well-endowed children to participate in activities outside school.

Column 7 shows a parameter estimate between those in columns 5 and 6, which implies that part of the downward bias is the result of measurement error attenuation, though the estimate is insignificant.

Grade Repetition

Table 4.7 summarizes the results on grade repetition. The dependent variable is the cumulative number of grades repeated. As in the previous section, all specifications include age fixed effects, which standardize years of repetition. Columns 1 and 2 show estimates with cluster and household fixed effects, respectively. The effect of the height z-score is insignificant in both cases. Consistent with the previous finding on grades completed, girls experience a smaller number of repetitions than boys.

Column 3 includes slope differences of the height-for-age z-score (as defined previously) to capture possible changes in the slope. These are found to be insignificant. In column 4 I include age interactions in addition to the slope differences. Interestingly, we find positive effects on grades repeated at ages 9 and 10 and height-for-age z-scores above 2. Though these results are only marginally significant, they are consistent with previous findings regarding grade completed.

In this chapter we cannot identify possible explanations for these findings. First, it is likely that for large children, ages were underreported in 1998, which leads to a positive estimate of the height effect among them. Second, we still cannot reject a hypothesis that the opportunity cost of schooling is high among large children because market and nonmarket returns to their health capital may be high.

Learning Outcomes

Table 4.8 reports the effects of height-for-age on mathematics test scores. In the 2004 survey we implemented four types of basic mathematics tests for children aged 7-9. For each question, an indicator is constructed to take the value of one if the answer is correct and zero otherwise (the descriptive statistics are given in Table 4.1).

Table 4.8 shows probit results with cluster fixed effects in columns 1-4.[20] Significantly positive effects are found in addition and subtraction—relatively easy computations. The point estimate decreases as the difficulty of calculation advances. In addition, age has a significant positive effect on the probability of answering correctly, which implies that schooling improves learning performance.

---

[20] Within-sibling estimation did not provide precise estimates owing to a small sample of children from households with multiple siblings in the 7-9 age group.

Table 4.7 Grade repetition

Explanatory variable	(1)	(2)	(3)	(4)
Haz	0.0126	0.0457	-0.0134	-0.0907
	(0.69)	(1.16)	(0.24)	(0.97)
Haz × I (Haz 2-6 years)			0.1390	0.2095
			(1.50)	(1.95)
Haz × age 8 years				-0.0119
				(0.11)
Haz × age 9 years				0.2390
				(1.71)
Haz × age 10 years				0.2120
				(1.88)
Haz × age 11 years				-0.0277
				(0.20)
Female	-0.2599	-0.3022	-0.3115	-0.2689
	(4.11)	(2.46)	(2.56)	(2.13)
Current age fixed effects	Yes	Yes	Yes	Yes
Cluster fixed effects	Yes			
Household fixed effects		Yes	Yes	Yes
Mean dependent variable	0.4336	0.4452	0.4452	0.4452
Mean Haz	-0.7170	-0.5106	-0.7170	-0.7170
Within-cluster R^2	0.1382			
Within-household R^2		0.2378	0.2599	0.3301
Number of children	399	155	155	155
Number of groups	60	71	71	71

Sources: University of KwaZulu-Natal / International Food Policy Research Institute / University of Wisconsin-Madison (1998, 2004).

Notes: Dependent variable is cumulative number of grades repeated. Numbers in parentheses are absolute *t*-values. Estimation with household (cluster) fixed effects uses children from households (clusters) with multiple children. Specifications include age fixed effects and over-age and under-age indicators for reported age in 1998. Sample consists of children aged 1-5 years, with consistent ages between 1998 and 2004, and height-for-age z-score in the range -6 to 6 in 1998. Haz means height-for-age z-score, 1998; I means indicator function.

Column 5 lists the number of total correct answers. Consistent with previous results, an increase in the height-for-age z-score as well as age improves learning performance. However, these estimates are potentially biased owing to omitted household factors, which are correlated with the height-for-age z-scores.

Outcomes at the Later Stage of Schooling

This section summarizes our findings on the effects of children's height-for-age z-score in 1993 on schooling outcomes in 2004. Before discussing the results, we note that South African education was in transition from apartheid to democ-

Table 4.8 Mathematical test results: Cluster fixed effects

	Probit				Linear
Explanatory variable	Addition (1)	Subtraction (2)	Multiplication (3)	Division (4)	Total correct (5)
Haz	0.1934	0.1363	0.0794	0.0579	0.1046
	(3.10)	(2.47)	(1.53)	(1.02)	(2.61)
Age 8 years in 2004	0.9223	0.6781	0.9498	0.6686	0.8148
	(3.49)	(2.94)	(3.92)	(2.22)	(4.54)
Age 9 years in 2004	1.3734	1.4401	1.8873	1.4923	1.4263
	(4.40)	(5.23)	(6.81)	(4.99)	(7.61)
Female	-0.0392	-0.2702	-0.2436	-0.1616	-0.1551
	(0.17)	(1.31)	(1.19)	(0.75)	(1.06)
Cluster fixed effects	Yes	Yes	Yes	Yes	Yes
Mean dependent variable	0.8169	0.6796	0.4507	0.1901	2.1373
Mean Haz	-0.7587	-0.7587	-0.7587	-0.7587	-0.7587
Pseudo R^2	0.2594	0.2210	0.2720	0.2092	
Within-cluster R^2					0.2192
Number of observations	209	239	235	224	284
Number of groups					54

Sources: University of KwaZulu-Natal / International Food Policy Research Institute / University of Wisconsin-Madison (1998, 2004).

Notes: Numbers in parentheses are absolute *t*-values. Sample consists of children aged 7–9 years in 2004 and with consistent ages between 1998 and 2004. Specifications include age fixed effects and over-age and under-age indicators for reported age in 1998. Though probit estimation with cluster dummies (columns 1–4) automatically omits observations from clusters in which it perfectly predicts the dependent variable, the computation of dependent and height-for-age z-score means includes those clusters. Haz means height-for-age z-score, 1998.

racy during the period 1993–98. The South African School Act and the Norms and Standards for School Funding were announced in 1996 and 1998, respectively; these introduced compulsory nonsegregated education throughout the system (although the reforms would take some time to have an effect).

It is also important to note that by 2004, this group of children was in transition from primary to secondary education. This may create heterogeneity by age in the effects of the height-for-age z-score on schooling outcomes. Therefore, it is important to examine possible variations in the height effect by age. The role of positive returns to health is expected to be greater among older children than younger children.

Table 4.9 shows the effects of the height-for-age z-score on grades completed and repeated. All the specifications control household fixed effects (using sibling variation within a household). Column 1 has only the height

Table 4.9 Grades completed and repeated, 1993 sample

	Grades completed			Grades repeated		
Explanatory variable	(1)	(2)	(3)	(4)	(5)	(6)
Haz	0.0545	0.2492	0.2388	0.0101	-0.1978	-0.1974
	(1.03)	(1.95)	(1.87)	(0.21)	(1.73)	(1.71)
Haz × age 12 years		-0.3639	-0.4111		0.1979	0.1995
		(2.21)	(2.44)		(1.35)	(1.32)
Haz × age 13 years		-0.2088	-0.2746		0.2157	0.2180
		(1.41)	(1.74)		(1.63)	(1.54)
Haz × age 14 years		-0.1016	-0.1537		0.3352	0.4085
		(0.56)	(0.83)		(2.07)	(1.46)
Haz × age 15 years		-0.2641	-0.3265		0.2771	0.2793
		(1.46)	(1.75)		(1.72)	(1.66)
Haz × age 16 years		-0.1004	-0.0870		0.2602	0.2598
		(0.44)	(0.39)		(1.25)	(1.25)
Haz × I (Haz 2-6 years)			0.1841			-0.0064
			(1.24)			(0.05)
Female	0.6023	0.6320	0.6492	-0.3798	-0.3907	-0.3913
	(4.05)	(4.19)	(4.30)	(2.86)	(2.89)	(2.87)
Age fixed effects	Yes	Yes	Yes	Yes	Yes	Yes
Household fixed effects	Yes	Yes	Yes	Yes	Yes	Yes
Mean dependent variable	6.4781	6.4781	6.4781	0.6764	0.6764	0.6764
Mean Haz	-0.9441	-0.9441	-0.9441	-0.9477	-0.9477	-0.9477
Within-household R^2	0.7689	0.7799	0.7825	0.1342	0.1685	0.1685
Number of children	251	251	251	247	247	247
Number of households	108	108	108	106	106	106

Sources: South African Labour and Development Research Unit, University of Cape Town (1994); University of KwaZulu-Natal / International Food Policy Research Institute / University of Wisconsin-Madison (1998, 2004).

Notes: Numbers in parentheses are absolute *t*-values. Estimation with household fixed effects uses children from households with multiple siblings. Specifications include age fixed effects and over-age and under-age indicators for reported age in 1993. Sample consists of children aged 0-5 years in 1993, with consistent ages between 1993 and 2004, and height-for-age z-score in the range -6 to 6 in 1993. Haz means height-for-age z-score, 1993; I means indicator function.

z-score, which shows its insignificance. Age heterogeneity is controlled in column 2. It is interesting to note again that an improvement in the height-for-age z-score marginally increases years of schooling completed, but it is likely to decrease grades completed as children age (conditional on age). Greater health capital may discourage further schooling from the primary stage to the secondary stage, given the positive returns to health in the labor market. It is also possible that height at ages older than 3 years may not have a positive direct effect on schooling attainment. To confirm the robustness of this finding, column 3 includes slope differences on the height-for-age z-score.

Contrary to the previous findings from younger children (and cohorts), nonlinearity is not found. We also find heterogeneity by age.

Columns 4–6 report on grade repetition. In column 5, similar to the results on grade completion, the height-for-age z-score has a negative effect among the youngest group (age 11), but the marginal effect becomes positive among older groups. This finding suggests that (conditional on age) greater health capital may discourage further investments in schooling at the transition from primary to secondary school. Column 6 investigates potential nonlinearity by introducing slope differences, which again show insignificant slope heterogeneity in grade repetition.[21]

In both grades completed and repeated, girls perform better than boys. However, a preliminary analysis shows that gender does not matter in the effect of the height-for-age z-score on these schooling outcomes (that is, the interaction is insignificant).

Summary

This chapter examined the effect of early-childhood health capital on schooling investments and outcomes, using panel data from South Africa. Good nutrition and health in early childhood are thought to be a precondition for child development and school learning at subsequent stages.

Nutrition intake and health capital in early childhood, measured by the height-for-age z-score of pre-primary-school-age children, enhance schooling investments and improve the outcomes. That is, children who are well nourished and in good health start school at an earlier age, progress further, and repeat fewer grades.

We also found that some taller children (z-scores above 2) perform worse than shorter children, but since the number of observations for this segment in our sample is very small and ages might have been underreported, it is difficult to generalize this nonlinearity. It is also important to note that different cohorts in our sample experienced certain historical changes in the South African education system, which might account for the age heterogeneity in the height effect.

[21] An alternative possibility is that the 1993 data are somehow flawed, causing these results. However, judging from the age consistency with the 2004 round, I conclude that the 1993 data are more accurate than the 1998 data.

CHAPTER 5

Impacts of Prime-Age Adult Mortality on Adolescents' Labor Supply

It is widely recognized that prime-age adult mortality has increased dramatically in many African countries. This drastic demographic change is largely attributed to the HIV/AIDS epidemic (for example, Epstein 2004). Excess mortality is concentrated among women between the ages of 25 and 39 and among men between the ages of 30 and 44 (Timaeus and Jasseh 2004). The micro foundations for such increases in adult mortality can be found in studies of the sexual activities and marriage decisions of young adults (Munshi and Myaux 2002; Hallman 2004; Oster 2005; Yamauchi 2007b; Ueyama and Yamauchi 2009).

Households can respond to an increase in mortality among prime-age adults in many ways. They can use government grants and formal insurance to smooth their income; they can engage in ex ante and ex post risk-coping or -mitigating strategies (for example, borrowing or relying on remittances) to buffer shocks; they can develop foster-care arrangements or income-diversification strategies). There are, however, problems with these approaches. If these strategies are imperfect in smoothing consumption, prime-age adult death can decrease child schooling investments and increase the labor supply, at least in the short run. Moreover, prime-age adult death also reduces the expected future earnings for the household. This in turn reduces investments in child schooling, given that the period over which capital is formed is long and the loan market is imperfect. Typically, growth in the number of orphans in a society is taxing on both families and the society (see Kelly 2000 quoted in Bennell 2005, 473), and an increase in mortality among prime-age adults, unlike mortality in other age groups, directly reduces the capability of households to secure income.

Motivated by recent increases in prime-age adult mortality in South Africa, we use recently available panel data to assess the impacts of such mortality on labor supply behavior in nonagricultural settings by examining the transition of adolescents from school to the labor market and examining female labor supply decisions.

The issue at hand in this chapter is of increasing importance to contemporary Africa. The death of adults in their productive years raises serious concerns about the pervasive impact of the HIV/AIDS epidemic on household behavior and on human capital development, particularly through education and labor supply decisions. Since the onset of HIV/AIDS more than two decades ago, mortality rates in many Sub-Saharan African countries have escalated dramatically. In South Africa, according to Statistics South Africa (2005), the number of annual recorded deaths in the 20–45 age group more than doubled between 1997 and 2002, from a little less than 90,000 to more than 190,000. Though *explicit* reports of HIV/AIDS as a cause of death are comparatively low, the number of HIV/AIDS deaths increases sharply when the underlying causes of the disease are taken into account: HIV/AIDS would account for nearly half of all deaths in South Africa (Groenewald et al. 2005). Over 70 percent of the deaths among those 15–49 years old can be attributed to HIV/AIDS, according to one model (Dorrington et al. 2006, ii, 21).

The next section, which deals with mortality changes, presents evidence of excess mortality among prime-age adults in the province of KwaZulu-Natal, using a particular dataset. The panel data I use throughout this chapter have been collected primarily from households in this province.

The main focus of our study is on adolescents' transition from school to the labor market and on changes in the time allocation between household production and labor-market activities, potentially as a response to prime-age adult mortality and as part of households' optimal risk-mitigation strategies. While I stress that responses to prime-age adult mortality are not only ex post but could also be ex ante (that is, before the adult's death), adult mortality would have a series of effects.[1] It has long-term implications for human capital formation if it causes an acceleration of adolescents' transition to the labor market (see, for example, Young 2005); in turn, to the extent that prime-age adult mortality produces children (for example, orphans) who cannot receive enough education and therefore participate in the labor market, HIV/AIDS creates inequalities in human capital (and earnings) between those affected and those unaffected.

[1] I have provided evidence (Yamauchi 2006) that marriage as an institution plays a role in mitigating AIDS risks; this implies that marriage could be an ex ante response to potential prime-age adult mortality. That paper shows that, because of interactions between marriage and labor markets, schooling may increase excess mortality among women, but not men. Along the same lines, Ueyama and Yamauchi (2009) report that marriage behavior has been changing in response to regional-level prime-age adult mortality shocks in Malawi.

On a shorter time horizon, the transition affects the unemployment rate among the young if, as a consequence of their exit from the school system, they are insufficiently educated. Another effect is on adult household members, who survive the crisis and accommodate the mortality shocks by changing their time allocation. For example, household members may need to look for earning opportunities in the labor market or may move to household work to care for the ill.[2] In the analysis that follows, I investigate these issues in detail, acknowledging the possibility that the behavioral response to adult mortality may differ by gender.

A number of recent studies attempt to identify the impacts of prime-age adult mortality on child schooling and labor supply (for example, Ainsworth, Beegle, and Koda 2005; Yamano and Jayne 2005). Though I subsequently detail the main relevant findings of these studies, and note that they vary greatly in their methodologies, the point is that they demonstrate the importance of prime-age adult deaths in determining child school enrollment and attendance. In the literature, however, the impact on labor supply is less visible than that on child schooling (Beegle 2005). Because we identify labor supply effects, our contribution to the literature is important in this regard. Also, whereas most of these studies share motivations similar to ours, they deal with agricultural settings. In contrast, our sample comes from semi-industrialized settings in South Africa, where the dominant income source for households is wage employment (see, for example, Dieden 2004). These differences provide a set of risk-coping and -mitigating strategies distinct from those in other rural contexts in Sub-Saharan Africa. They also justify our focus on labor supply and schooling decisions.

This chapter is structured as follows. The section "Mortality Change" provides evidence of excess mortality in the province of KwaZulu-Natal. The data used for this chapter come from KIDS rounds 2 and 3, conducted in 1998 and 2004, respectively. "Impact of Prime-Age Adult Mortality on Schooling and Labor Supply" sets the empirical framework for our analysis. The next two sections respectively describe activity transitions in the sample and present our empirical results.

---

[2] Though these phenomena occur at the micro level, it is often argued at the macro level that prime-age adult mortality resulting from HIV/AIDS causes labor shortages. However, with high unemployment rates, as observed in South Africa, labor shortages may not occur if the degree of (skill) substitutability between the dying and the unemployed is high. Even in agricultural household production, where this causality looks rather straightforward, the degree of substitution between household members and hired labor matters. However, if female household members engage in a shift, there might then be a decrease in their time input to child education in the family. Therefore, changes in labor supply might affect human capital formation over the medium run.

Several findings emerge from the analysis. I find first that deaths of prime-age working adults significantly increase the labor supply of both male and female adolescents, stopping their schooling. Deaths of prime-age adults in the future decrease female school enrollment, suggesting that girls shift activity, possibly staying at home to take care of the sick or of the household more generally. Second, since the enrollment of male adolescents is decreased prior to the death of a *working* adult, their response is different, intended to compensate for an income loss. These findings imply that excess mortality among prime-age adults disrupts human capital formation in the society.

Mortality Change

The 2004 KIDS data allow us to link death with specific changes among household members, because the data contain retrospective information on those who died between 1998 and 2004. More specifically, the data allow an identification of the individuals who died and when the death occurred. (However, to minimize emotional distress, respondents were not asked about deaths when these had occurred up to three months prior to the 2004 survey.) Combining this information with the roster information on individuals in 1998, I can identify the age at death. This information is critical for our analysis as it enables us to identify changes over the period 1998–2004. This corresponds to the time when South Africa experienced substantial increases in prime-age adult mortality (for example, Groenewald et al. 2005; Statistics South Africa 2005). In other words, the period covered is quite appropriate to identify the impacts of prime-age adult mortality on the time allocation decisions of children and housewives.

Figures 5.1 and 5.2 show the changes in mortality rates between 1998 and 2004 for the populations of males and of females, respectively. One of the two series plotted on the figures presents information gathered from the surveyed households. The changes are reported across age groups. Each figure illustrates the non-AIDS mortality rate for South Africa as one of the two series. These data are from the 2002 model estimates of the Actuarial Society of South Africa (ASSA) for 1996 and for all racial groups. Data for 1996 were chosen to provide a credible non-AIDS mortality rate relative to the period spanned by the KIDS data. Age-specific non-AIDS mortality rates for men and women are the benchmark rates against which the KIDS mortality rates—the second data series in Figures 5.1 and 5.2—are considered in this section (see Table 5.1). Since the sample period I consider spans six years, the mortality rate of the KIDS household members over the period is converted into annual terms assuming a constant mortality rate throughout the period. The two figures show significant increases in adult mortality for those aged 20-44 across gender—the gap between the two lines in the two figures reflects

Figure 5.1 Mortality rate: Male

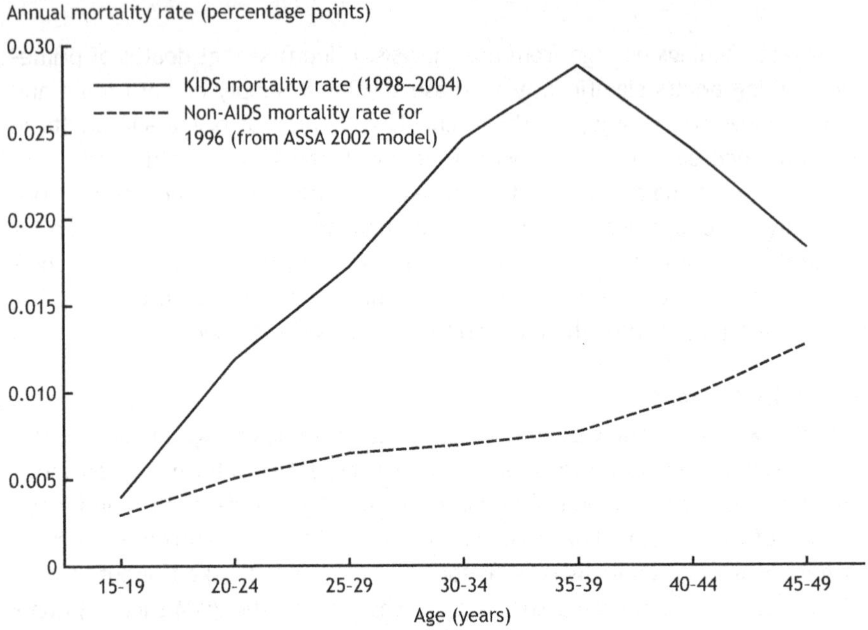

Sources: Actuarial Society of South Africa (2002); University of KwaZulu-Natal / International Food Policy Research Institute / University of Wisconsin-Madison (1998, 2004).

Figure 5.2 Mortality rate: Female

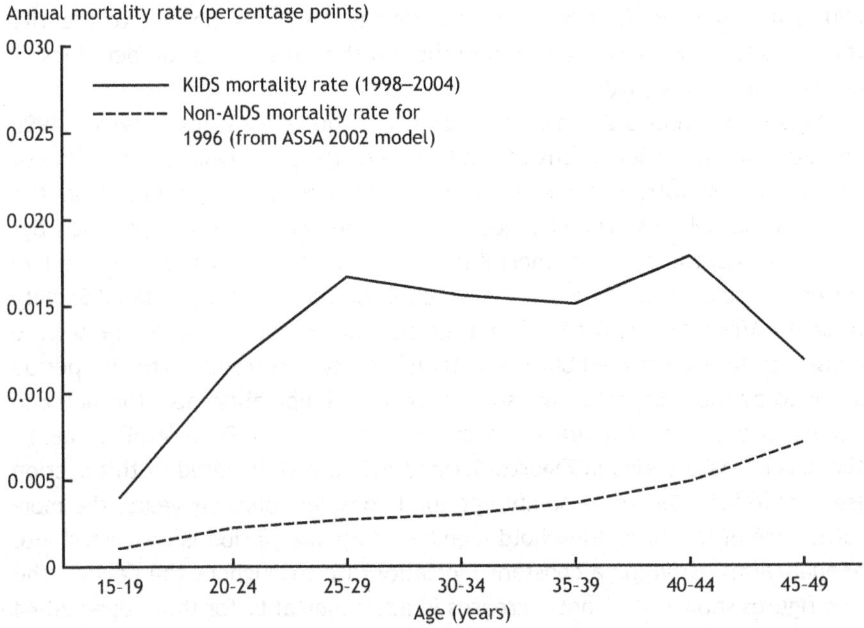

Sources: Actuarial Society of South Africa (2002); University of KwaZulu-Natal / International Food Policy Research Institute / University of Wisconsin-Madison (1998, 2004).

excess mortality in the KIDS sample at the end of the 1990s for each age group. The figures also show that excess mortality is higher for males than for females.[3]

Table 5.1 reports the probit results on individual-level mortality, controlling for the age-specific non-AIDS mortality rates. The non-AIDS mortality rate is that from the ASSA 2002 model. This variable is included to control for the pre-AIDS level of mortality rate. The various results incorporate cluster fixed effects (columns 1-4), allow for household random effects (columns 5-7), and finally incorporate household fixed effects (columns 8-10).

Column 1 reports the results using only the non-AIDS mortality rate and a gender dummy. The results confirm that the benchmark non-AIDS level of mortality significantly explains mortality over the period 1998-2004, though the gender dummy is insignificant. Column 2 introduces age-group indicators to capture age-specific changes in mortality during the period. With those aged 15-19 as the omitted group, we find significant increases in mortality among those aged 20-44. Households faced some exogenous changes in prime-age adult mortality among those aged 20-44 over the period. To distinguish age-specific mortality changes between men and women, columns 3 and 4 report the results of separate estimations by gender. The results show that there are larger increases in mortality among men than among women, particularly among men aged 30 and older. However, during the period under study, those aged 20-44 experienced significant increases in mortality across both groups.

Given that these findings might have been generated by unobservable household-specific factors correlated with the household demographic structure, I alter the model specifications. Columns 5-7 report the results of probit regressions for the within-household incidence of mortality with household random effects. Columns 8-10 use household fixed effects in linear models. Both the random-effect and fixed-effect estimates show qualitatively similar effects of the age indicators and individual characteristics. Yet the significance of parameter estimates in the fixed-effect estimates is slightly lower than that for the random-effect probit results.

These results are important: they confirm that those between 20 and 44 years of age in 1998 were more likely to die than others in each household. Increases in the incidence of mortality among the prime-age adults should cause a reallocation of resources within the household, including changes in time allocation among household members. This effect arises as household members seek to mitigate the negative impacts of adult mortality on household welfare.

---

[3] It is generally agreed that female mortality is higher than that for males. It is possible that male migrant workers came back home to die, which increases the estimate of the excess mortality rate in our sample.

Table 5.1 Mortality changes, 1998-2004

	Probit				Household random-effects probit			Household fixed-effects linear		
Explanatory variable	Both male and female (1)	Both male and female (2)	Male (3)	Female (4)	Both male and female (5)	Male (6)	Female (7)	Both male and female (8)	Male (9)	Female (10)
Non-AIDS mortality rate, 1996	34.197	48.252	37.986	46.188	46.437	53.384	59.445	11.008	-2.5718	7.5971
	(7.64)	(2.65)	(0.92)	(0.79)	(2.62)	(1.41)	(1.00)	(2.74)	(0.21)	(0.52)
Ages 20-24 years		0.4246	0.4568	0.4582	0.4069	0.3794	0.4045	0.0251	0.0729	0.0532
		(3.50)	(2.44)	(2.60)	(3.52)	(2.10)	(2.43)	(1.77)	(2.08)	(2.26)
Ages 25-29 years		0.5641	0.5870	0.6014	0.5663	0.5106	0.5700	0.0342	0.0966	0.0603
		(4.38)	(2.72)	(3.24)	(4.78)	(2.48)	(3.31)	(1.84)	(1.89)	(1.95)
Ages 30-34 years		0.6327	0.7737	0.5987	0.6328	0.6722	0.5462	0.0517	0.1191	0.0643
		(4.69)	(3.27)	(2.96)	(5.05)	(3.03)	(2.89)	(2.39)	(2.02)	(1.81)
Ages 35-39 years		0.6664	0.9305	0.5589	0.6182	0.7383	0.4472	0.0556	0.1903	0.0324
		(4.73)	(3.51)	(2.53)	(4.62)	(2.99)	(2.09)	(2.45)	(2.77)	(0.80)
Ages 40-44 years		0.5567	0.7130	0.5073	0.5266	0.4832	0.4762	0.0442	0.1243	0.0718
		(3.32)	(2.11)	(1.74)	(3.34)	(1.54)	(1.71)	(1.51)	(1.34)	(1.17)

Ages 45-49 years		0.2607	0.4213	0.2142	0.2215	0.1940	0.1053	-0.0345	0.0710	-0.0085
		(1.26)	(0.92)	(0.55)	(1.13)	(0.46)	(0.27)	(0.99)	(0.57)	(0.10)
Ages 50-54 years		0.2395	0.4024	0.2941	0.1929	0.0339	0.1292	-0.0418	0.1930	-0.0278
		(0.85)	(0.59)	(0.51)	(0.72)	(0.05)	(0.22)	(0.79)	(0.98)	(0.21)
Ages 55-59 years		0.2379	0.3491	0.4034	0.1886	-0.0891	0.1482	-0.0554	0.2322	0.0090
		(0.64)	(0.38)	(0.49)	(0.54)	(0.10)	(0.18)	(0.74)	(0.89)	(0.05)
Ages 60-64 years		-0.0358	0.4655	-0.0924	0.0121	-0.0697	-0.3428	-0.1171	0.4348	-0.0510
		(0.08)	(0.37)	(0.08)	(0.03)	(0.06)	(0.30)	(1.25)	(1.16)	(0.19)
Male	0.0155	-0.0357			-0.0413			-0.0095		
	(0.29)	(0.37)			(0.42)			(0.55)		
Cluster fixed effects	Yes	Yes	Yes	Yes						
Household random effects					Yes	Yes	Yes			
Household fixed effects								Yes	Yes	Yes
Number of observations	4,532	4,532	1,950	2,272	4,549	2,086	2,509	4,549	2,086	2,509
Pseudo R^2	0.0557	0.0770	0.1081	0.0637	n.a.	n.a.	n.a.	n.a.	n.a.	n.a.

Sources: Actuarial Society of South Africa (2002); University of KwaZulu-Natal / International Food Policy Research Institute / University of Wisconsin-Madison (1998, 2004).

Notes: The dependent variable is height-for-age *z*-score. The dependent variable equals one if the individual died during the interval 1998-2004 and zero if he or she was alive in 2004. Numbers in parentheses are absolute asymptotic *t*-values, using robust standard errors with household clusters. The non-AIDS mortality rate for 1996 is taken from the 2002 model estimates of the Actuarial Society of South Africa. Sample consists of those aged 15-64 years in 1998. n.a. means not available.

Impact of Prime-Age Adult Mortality on Schooling and Labor Supply

Prime-Age Adult Mortality and Labor Supply

A handful of studies examine the impact of prime-age adult mortality on labor supply. With the HIV/AIDS epidemic striking most men and women at their prime age, an investigation of this phenomenon remains a necessity in developing countries generally and in South Africa in particular. Some studies focus on this impact in countries where the labor supply is largely within the agricultural sector. In contrast, very few studies examine this impact within the nonagricultural sector. The key focus of this chapter is the examination of changes in the time allocation of adolescents who experience prime-age adult death or illness in their households. In order to smooth household consumption and income, adolescents exit school and enter the labor market (whether employed or unemployed), and female household members alter their labor force participation.

A few studies empirically examine the impact of AIDS mortality on labor supply. An analysis of two LFSs (1990–91 and 2000–01) in Tanzania undertaken by Wobst and Arndt (2004) revealed an important trend in this regard; the data suggest a dramatic increase in labor force participation rates for children aged 10–14, from 23 percent to 46 percent, implying a tendency to exit primary schools over the decade. This chapter is similar to their paper in that I focus on adolescents' time allocation. However, I explore this issue using micro-longitudinal data instead of the aggregate measures that are used in their analysis.

There are two studies on this topic from dominantly agrarian settings: Beegle (2005) and Donovan et al. (2003). Using panel data from Tanzania, Beegle (2005) explores how prime-age adult mortality affects the time allocation of surviving household members and the portfolio of household farming activities. The author analyzes hours spent farming and on household chores across demographic groups and finds small and insignificant changes in the labor supply of individuals in households that experience a prime-age adult death. While some farm activities are temporarily scaled back and wage employment falls after a male death, households did not shift cultivation away from subsistence farming. Moreover, they did not appear to reduce their diversification of income sources more than six months after a death.

Donovan et al. (2003) analyze the effects of prime-age adult morbidity and mortality in rural Rwanda using recent data from household surveys with overlapping samples and retrospective information on deaths within the household. They show that loss of agricultural labor was most pronounced for tasks involving cropping and animal husbandry relative to other potential effects (for example, diet effects, effects on children, and other income-generating effects).

Our empirical setting is different from that of these two studies in that most of the sample households supply labor in nonagricultural sectors. That is, intrahousehold decisions on labor allocation for self-employment, such as own farming, are not the issue. With a focus on trade-offs between human capital investments and labor supply, I analyze labor force participation decisions among adolescents without distinguishing between the agricultural and nonagricultural sectors.

Prime-Age Adult Mortality and Child Schooling

It is widely believed that the death of a parent and prime-age household member has serious repercussions on the well-being and future of children—their schooling in particular. However, the literature on this topic does not necessarily present similar results, partly because of differences in methodologies across studies.

First, the literature is divided into two groups of studies: those using panel data and those based on cross-sectional data. The studies that used panel data can potentially identify ex ante and ex post effects of prime-age adult mortality on child schooling.

Second, the focus of studies may be parental deaths (leading to orphanhood) or prime-age adult deaths in general. Since the two are not exclusive, studies could basically analyze both impacts, but this portion of the literature is generally divided into two groups, with relative emphasis on either parental deaths or prime-age deaths. This chapter sheds light on both issues using panel data.

Approaches and findings from the literature are summarized in Table 5.2.

Five studies use panel data: Ainsworth, Beegle, and Koda (2005); Yamano and Jayne (2005); Beagle, De Weerdt, and Dercon (2006); Case and Ardington (2006); and Evans and Miguel (2007). All of these studies, except Beegle, De Weerdt, and Dercon (2006), used standard methods of panel analysis with children in similar age ranges. Beegle, De Weerdt, and Dercon (2006) used children aged 0-15 who had not experienced parental deaths in the baseline to track their completed years of schooling and anthropometric measures later in their lives, under the assumption that parental deaths were not predictable and also not correlated with the health and schooling of children in the initial round. In this respect, although they used panel data, it is not straightforward to compare their results with others.

As Table 5.2 shows, with the exception of Yamano and Jayne (2005), all studies analyzed the effects of parental deaths. However, Ainsworth, Beegle, and Koda (2005) and Yamano and Jayne (2005) are the only studies that directly

Table 5.2 Literature summary: Impacts of prime-age deaths on child schooling

Study	Data type	Child age group (years)	Measures	Orphanhood	Prime-age adult death	Ex ante impacts	Ex post impacts	Main findings
Case, Paxson, and Ableidinger (2004)	Cross-section	6-14	Enrollment	Yes (within household)	No	n.a.	n.a.	Orphans lower than non-orphans in the same household
Ainsworth, Beegle, and Koda (2005)	Panel	7-14	Attendance Hours at school (panel)	Yes	Yes	Yes	Yes	Hours at school: ex ante effect
Yamano and Jayne (2005)	Panel	7-14	Attendance	No	Yes	Yes	Yes	Ex ante effect
Ainsworth and Filmer (2006)	Cross-section	7-14	Enrollment	Yes	No	n.a.	n.a.	Not clear
Beegle, De Weerdt, and Dercon (2006)	Panel	0-15 (baseline 11-28 in 2004)[a]	Years of schooling	Yes	No	Yes	Yes	Both parents combined: significant (but depends on specifications and age group)
Case and Ardington (2006)	Panel	6-16	Years of schooling Enrollment Log monthly expense	Yes	No	Yes	Yes	Maternal death: significant Paternal death: insignificant
Evans and Miguel (2007)	Panel	5-18 (grades 1-7)	School participation	Yes	No	Yes	Yes	Maternal death: both ex ante and ex post effects Both parents combined: ex post effect significant
Ardington and Leibbrandt (2010)	Cross-section	8-17	Years of schooling Enrollment	Yes (within household)	No	n.a.	n.a.	Maternal death effect larger

Note: n.a. means not available.
[a]Non-orphan sample from the baseline.

analyzed the effects of prime-age adult deaths. In all studies, both ex ante and ex post impacts are studied.

Of the two studies that highlight the effects of prime-age adult mortality, both report that the ex ante effect of prime-age adult deaths—hours at school in Ainsworth, Beegle, and Koda (2005) and school attendance in Yamano and Jayne (2005)—is significantly negative. As discussed subsequently, our results also show significant ex ante effects on adolescents' transition from school to labor markets (that is, changes in enrollment status).

The other studies which focus on parental deaths (Case and Ardington 2006; Evans and Miguel 2007) show that a mother's death has a more significant and strongly negative impact on child schooling than a father's death. This chapter, however, shows that both mothers' and fathers' deaths have almost equal impacts on adolescents' decisions regarding the continuation of schooling.

One caveat in these comparisons arises from differences in the child age range between the present study and the other studies in the literature (see the third column in Table 5.2). In our sample from South Africa, enrollment status does not show any cross-sectional variations among children below age 13 at the primary-school level, partly because of the tendency of children to remain enrolled even if they participate in some other activities. In this sense, more sophisticated measures of schooling, such as attendance, should be used, but I decided not to pursue this line of investigation since the 1998 data do not include such information.

Three studies used cross-sectional data: Case, Paxson, and Ableidinger (2004), Ainsworth and Filmer (2006), and Ardington and Leibbrandt (2010). Case, Paxson, and Ableidinger (2004) and Ardington and Leibbrandt (2010) used within-household variations to address the relative status of orphans who lost their parent(s). The former study shows that orphans' enrollment is lower than that of non-orphans within the same household, though residence arrangement is an endogenous choice. If orphans become better off by moving into other households (for example, those of relatives who have not experienced parental death) after losing their parent(s), their status is overestimated in this method—which, however, only strengthens the findings. Using within-household variations, Ardington and Leibbrandt (2010) found that maternal death has a larger effect on years of schooling and enrollment than paternal death—a finding in line with those from other studies using panel data.

Ainsworth and Filmer's (2006) results are not clear. Using data from 51 countries, they report that orphans' enrollment status is not significantly lower than that of non-orphans in many countries—but as they acknowledge, this could be attributed to the failure in their methodology to account for socioeconomic factors that determine orphan status.

Our approach belongs to the first group of studies, those using panel data. Owing to data constraints (explained earlier), I focus on the enrollment status of adolescents aged 14–19 in the baseline and their transitions to labor markets thereafter. Though our results in general conform to those in the literature, one difference is the finding of almost equal magnitudes of ex post effects of maternal and paternal deaths, partly as a result of difference in the age ranges used. Because of small incidences of parental deaths in a short period, it was not possible to estimate the ex ante effects.

Framework

Specification and Estimation

This section describes our empirical methodology. The behavioral equation of interest to us is as follows:

$$y^*_{ijt} = \alpha + x_{jt}\beta + \gamma s_{it0} + \delta a_{it0} + \mu_{ij} + \varepsilon_{ijt}, \tag{5.1}$$

where, for individual i in household j at time t, our observable activity indicator y_{ijt} = 1 (enrolled in school or engaged in housework) if latent variable $y^*_{ijt} \geq 0$ and y_{ijt} = 0 (in labor market) otherwise, x_{jt} is a vector of household-level factors including the demographic composition of the household, s_{it0} is the highest grade completed in the initial period t_0, a_{it0} is age at the initial period t_0, μ_{ij} is individual i's fixed effect in household j, and ε_{ijt} follows the standard normal cumulative distribution function (probit) or the logistic cumulative distribution function (logit). As I discuss subsequently, I use conditional logit estimation to eliminate time-invariant factors in the analysis of dynamic activity transition.[4]

Although schooling level and age in the initial period are controlled for in equation (5.1), these time-invariant variables in addition to unobserved fixed effects do not contribute to the estimation of the transition equation. Therefore, in the estimations carried out next I include initial age and schooling fixed effects only when estimating the prime-age adult mortality effect in cross-sectional models to control for potential unobserved heterogeneity of labor supply behavior attributable to predetermined schooling attainment and age.[5]

[4] Although multinomial logit estimation is also applicable in this context to capture participation in (1) school (adolescents) or housework (adult females), (2) the labor market, and (3) other activities, I decided to focus on (1) and (2) since the number of observations for (3) is very small in our sample of individuals in specific age ranges. The inclusion of observations for other activities destabilizes the parameter estimates in maximum likelihood estimation.

[5] Including both initial schooling and age fixed effects indirectly controls for the effect of past grade repetitions on the labor supply.

Correlations between x_{jt} and μ_i bias estimates of β. To solve this problem, I focus on changes in activity (for example, transitions from school to the labor market) over time. More specifically, I adopt the conditional (fixed-effect) logit model to eliminate μ_{ij} (Chamberlain 1984).[6] The process involves first differencing the right-hand-side variables, which produces Δx_j. This term captures changes in households' demographic composition; in our setting it represents the death of prime-age adult members.

Potential Endogeneity of Prime-Age Adult Mortality

The endogeneity of adult mortality is not perfectly resolved, as we may potentially have $E[\Delta x_j \varepsilon_{i1}] = E[x_{j2}\varepsilon_{i1}] \neq 0$. (See also Beegle 2005 for a detailed discussion of potential endogeneity problems of adult deaths.) To illustrate the problem, we can take the example of a drop in household income that is caused by a death and which causes dropouts from school in a context of credit constraints. The income drop at the initial stage could worsen subsequent living conditions. The worsened living conditions can, in turn, contribute to adult mortality. Therefore, the income drop can cause adult mortality and child dropouts from school.

Ex Ante Response, Selectivity, and Transition

In the case of HIV/AIDS-related mortality, it is possible that foreseeing the death of AIDS-infected family members causes other members to adjust to the negative impacts ex ante, for instance by increasing the labor supply to secure the household's income. The question is who in the household changes his or her time allocation along with the shocks. For example, if girls are more likely than boys to care for the sick at home, girls' enrollment rate should be lower than that of boys even before the death of the ill family member(s).[7] I use a sample of individuals aged 14-19 in 1998 irrespective of their enrollment status to check for ex ante responses.

---

[6] The estimation uses the joint distribution of the dependent variable conditional on the explanatory variables, the fixed component, and the sum of the dependent variable over time (in this case, 0, 1, and 2). The conditional distribution does not depend on the fixed component. I therefore do not estimate fixed effects in the conditional logit model.

[7] If some household members (including school-age children) have already changed their time allocation as they anticipate the death of some adult members, it would not be necessary for other members to accommodate the negative impacts of adult death by making additional changes in time allocation decisions. This would lead to an underestimation of the impacts on labor supply and on schooling in our framework. We have not detected a causal link between enrollment in the initial period and the number of prime-age adult deaths in the following six years. In parts of the subsequent data analysis we examine the effect of future adult death (over a three-year time span) on initial-period enrollment by gender.

Although it is not possible in this data to identify whether a transition out of school is temporary, most adolescent transitions are a one-way process in our empirical setting. Though those who were recorded as participating in labor-force activities do not move back to school after the six-year interval covered by our panel data, the fact that I ignore the heterogeneity in the initial state causes a selectivity bias in the estimates. Therefore, I do not restrict the sample to those who were enrolled in school but also incorporate those already in the labor market in 1998. I also investigate how future mortality affects the initial state. If household members anticipate the death, in the future, of a household member, they may adjust their behavior ex ante to accommodate for the negative shocks that arise ex post.[8] Finally, in the analysis of adult labor supply, I focus on women's time allocation between in-house and labor-market activities.

Activity Transitions

The KIDS surveys provide information about the activities of household members by employment status; labor force status consists of three categories of employment (regular employment, casual or temporary employment, self-employment) as well as unemployment. The KIDS data also specify whether an individual is unemployed, a "housewife / involved with child care," in school (including at a university), at a crèche or preprimary school, retired, or "other." The specifications are obtained from the respondents themselves. Although it is not possible to verify in the dataset whether the respondents are actively seeking employment, school enrollment and unemployment are mutually exclusive among the questionnaire options. Combining the two survey rounds, it is possible to establish the transitions in activity from 1998 to 2004, although details of activities within the intervening period are not available.

Table 5.3 shows the activity transitions from 1998 to 2004 among adolescents, that is, for those aged 14–19 in 1998.[9] Two main trends emerge from the data. First, it is interesting to find that among those who transitioned to the labor market, the majority were unemployed in 2004. As discussed in

[8] Given the survey interval of three years (1998–2004), my measurement of ex ante actions is not perfect in the sense that the 1998 data probably only captured ex ante actions for events that were occurring a few years ahead (say, 1998–2001). Similarly, ex post actions must have occurred before 2004 if events occurred immediately after 1998. However, the 2004 data are likely to capture these ex ante actions if they were not reversible.

[9] In my empirical analysis, I target adolescents aged 14–19 in the initial period. Thus my results on schooling can be qualitatively different from those of other studies. In particular, I do not find that a mother's death has a larger adverse impact on child schooling than a father's death. I find that the death of working males has a large impact on adolescents' schooling (labor supply) decisions.

Table 5.3 Activity transitions, individuals aged 14-19 years, 1998-2004

	Activity 2004 (row percentages)							
Activity 1998	Regular employment	Casual employment	Self-employment	Housewife / child rearing	Unemployed	Education	Total 1998 (%)	Total cases, 1998
Education (school)								
Ages 14-19 years	5.3	10.2	1.5	0.9	50.4	31.8	100	548
Male	2.4	6.0	0.9	0	23.9	17.2	50.4	276
Female	2.9	4.2	0.5	0.9	26.5	14.6	49.6	272

Sources: University of KwaZulu-Natal / International Food Policy Research Institute / University of Wisconsin-Madison (1998, 2004).
Note: Ages are as of 1998.

Chapter 1, this tendency reflects current labor-market conditions in South Africa, where the unemployment rate is high, particularly among the young. It is important to note that making the transition from school to the labor markets does not necessarily mean that individuals are employed in those markets. In the analysis that follows, I examine adolescents' transitions from education to the labor force, including both employment and unemployment.

Second, the transition from school to the labor force occurs in a relatively similar manner for both men and women. In South Africa gender gaps in schooling investment and in labor markets are relatively unimportant.

The 1998 data contain seven adolescents whose activities were not classified as either labor market or school. Since the number of observations in this group is small, I decided not to show them in the table. The analysis in the next section also excludes this group, as inclusion of them in a multinomial logit analysis makes the estimation unstable. In the next section I provide empirical results on the impact of prime-age adult death on adolescents' decisions to continue with schooling or to enter the labor market.

Empirical Results: Adolescent Transitions to Labor Markets

I use prime-age adult mortality as a measure of AIDS-induced mortality shocks to households in the analysis of adolescents' transitions from school to labor markets. An alternative method is to use parental death. These choices are not exclusive, but they could shed light on different aspects of AIDS-related mortality.

In our sample, I had 408 cases of prime-age adult mortality (defined for ages 15-64). Among the children aged 14-19 who were residing in the sample households in 1998, 43 children lost their mothers during the interval 1998-2004, and 60 lost their fathers.[10] The number of children who had already lost their parent(s) before 1998 is not included in these figures, so the number of orphans is greater. A total of 362 children experienced prime-age adult mortality in their households.[11]

In this chapter, though I focus on the impacts of prime-age adult mortality, it is also interesting to examine the impacts of parental deaths and compare the results. As discussed in the previous section, the literature seems to confirm that a mother's death has a significantly greater adverse impact on

[10] The numbers of children who lost their mothers and fathers are 35 and 46, respectively, if we restrict the sample to ages 15-64.

[11] During the period 1998-2004, 444 children experienced deaths in their households. Of these, 125 children experienced the loss of working prime-age adults. There were 18 cases of deaths among the children aged 14-19. These cases are not included in the panel data, so we are examining the effects on other siblings. This sample is small relative to the total sample of children aged 14-19.

child schooling than a father's death. This finding does not contradict the hypothesis that the death of a prime-age adult (especially one who is working, and thus contributing to household income) has a negative effect on child schooling. In fact I also confirm in this study that a mother's death has an equal and significant negative impact on child schooling for boys and girls.

In this section I detail the main findings on the impact of prime-age adult mortality on the time allocation of adolescents. In the analysis that follows, I use two different definitions of prime-age adults: those between the ages of 20 and 64, and those between the ages of 20 and 44. The former corresponds mainly to the age range for labor force participation, while the latter focuses on the age range in which, as shown in the section "Mortality Change," I found substantial increases in mortality rate.[12] I consider a variety of measures of prime-age adult mortality—the total number of deaths in the household, prime-age adult deaths (ages 20–64 or 20–44), and deaths of working members and of prime-age working adult members, differentiated by gender and occurring between 1998 and 2004—as explanatory variables. For the data, I do not capture deaths of members who moved out of the households.[13] Instead, I include occurrences of death of new members who moved into the households, which have a relatively smaller effect on time allocation decisions. Mortality estimates could accordingly be biased in either direction.[14]

Table 5.4 shows how prime-age adult mortality in the very near future, 1998–2001, affects school enrollment in 1998, that is, ex ante. If future mortality among prime-age adults in the household is preceded by the need for home care, additional incomes, or both, it may change the time allocation of adolescents.[15] Since this analysis is cross-sectional, I include initial grade and

[12] There are some reservations. First, although the age range 15–64 is a standard definition of members of a population in the labor force, we may potentially miss the effects of deaths among the elderly who were receiving pensions from the government. Second, as discussed subsequently, there were 18 children aged 14–19 (as of the 1998 survey) who died in the period 1998–2004. I do not include these adolescents in the analysis, but the effects of their deaths on their siblings are included. Third, labor market employment among those aged 15 and 16 is rare, but since the focus of our analysis is on their transition to the labor market, whether or not they are employed is not directly relevant.

[13] In the South African context, owing to the extensive use of migrant labor, it is often someone outside the household who takes responsibility for supporting child schooling. In this case, mortality in the household may not matter. In other words, we have strong evidence if we find a significant negative effect on adolescents' schooling.

[14] Even though tracking individuals who moved away from survey sites was extensively attempted, it was necessary to drop from the analysis individuals who have died as well as those who could not be found. In considering the selectivity problem that may arise from mortality during the period, the results for adolescents aged 14–19 are robust to prime-age adult mortality in general, and those for female adults are robust to prime-age male adult deaths.

[15] Ainsworth, Beegle, and Koda (2005) and Yamano and Jayne (2005) conducted similar analyses on ex ante behavior. Our results largely confirm their findings.

Table 5.4 Impact of future mortality on adolescent enrollment, 1998

Explanatory variable	(1)	(2)	(3)	(4)	(5)	(6)
Prime-age deaths (20-64 years)	0.1546	0.1653				
	(0.50)	(0.53)				
Prime-age working deaths (20-64 years)	-0.9943	-0.6800				
	(2.02)	(1.06)				
× Male		-0.8699				
		(1.19)				
Prime-age deaths (20-44 years)			-0.6470	-0.2600		
			(2.50)	(0.86)		
× Male				-1.0060		
				(2.18)		
Male prime-age deaths (20-44 years)					-0.0674	0.5184
					(0.19)	(1.17)
× Male						-1.3810
						(2.30)
Female prime-age deaths (20-44 years)					-1.1911	-0.8935
					(3.35)	(1.91)
× Male						-0.8477
						(1.31)
Number of observations	524	524	524	524	524	524
Pseudo R^2	0.4291	0.4316	0.4313	0.4380	0.4417	0.4495

Sources: University of KwaZulu-Natal / International Food Policy Research Institute / University of Wisconsin-Madison (1998, 2004).

Notes: The dependent variable equals one if the individual was in school in 1998 and zero otherwise. Probit estimation used. The numbers in parentheses are absolute z-values. Robust standard errors are used with household-level clusters. The sample uses individuals aged 14-19 years in 1998, with the highest completed years of schooling strictly above zero. All specifications also include age in 1998; the value of durable goods in 1998; the number of household members in 1998 in age groups 0-4, 5-9, 10-14, 15-19, 20-24, 25-29, 30-34, 35-39, 40-44, 45-49, 50-54, 55-59, 60-64, and 65 years or above who have lived more than 15 days in the household in the previous month; and both grade (1998) and cluster fixed effects. Except for cluster fixed effects, these variables are interacted with a male dummy. The specifications include parental deaths in 1998-2001, but the effect was not estimable because of the small incidences of parental deaths in the three-year period 1998-2001.

cluster (community) dummies and age to control observable heterogeneity, possibly determining schooling progression and transition to the labor market. Since in our sample all children under age 13 were enrolled in schools, I do not include those children.

Column 1 includes deaths of prime-age (20-64) members and prime-age working members. In the preliminary analysis, I included mother's and father's deaths in 1998-2001, but the number of observations is so few that it was not feasible to estimate their effects. Adding both values to arrive at total parental deaths did not help estimate their effects.

The prime-age (20-64) deaths on their own do not affect enrollment significantly, but those of working members significantly decrease enrollment.

Given a significant ex ante negative effect on enrollment of the future death of a working adult of prime age, I can conclude that male adolescents' labor supply is likely to increase when the household income drops as a result of the death of a working adult. Column 2 adds the interaction of working prime-age deaths at ages 20–64 and a male adolescent dummy. However, I do not find any significant effects in this specification.

In column 3 I use the prime-age definition of 20–44 years to account for the fact that this group has experienced significant excess mortality (see Table 5.1 and Figures 5.1 and 5.2). This measure is highly correlated with the death of working prime-age (20–64) members. The results in columns 1 and 2 indicate that the deaths of working prime-age adults active at ages 20–44, which cause a reduction of household income, have larger and more significant impacts on adolescents' transition to labor markets.

Column 4 disaggregates the prime-age (20–44) death effects by adolescents' gender. First, though the prime-age (20–44) adult deaths did not affect enrollment in general, we find that they significantly decreased males' enrollment. However, the effect is significantly negative for male adolescents. This finding suggests that male adolescents assume greater responsibility for supporting their households by moving from school to labor markets once a prime-age adult dies.

In column 5 I consider deaths of male and female prime-age (20–44) household members separately. Interestingly, the effect of female deaths is significantly negative while that of male deaths is insignificant. I further decompose the effect by distinguishing between male and female adolescents (column 6). The deaths of male prime-age members significantly decrease male adolescents' schooling, but not that of female adolescents. However, the deaths of female prime-age members decrease both male and female adolescents' schooling (thus promoting their transition to labor markets).

Since the analysis is cross-sectional, we cannot distinguish the preceding interpretation from the case in which these females live in households with certain characteristics that are more likely to result in an adult death (that is, poor households). To account for this, I included the value of durable goods (assets) in 1998 in the regressions.

In this analysis I also tried to expand the sample by including younger children (age below 13) as part of the robustness checks, but since almost all children in this age range were enrolled in schools, this change does not improve the precision of the estimates.[16]

[16] On the high enrollment rate among African learners, see also Lam, Ardington, and Leibbrandt (2009).

Case, Paxson, and Ableidinger (2004) and Case and Ardington (2006) indicate that male death is likely to occur in poor households. If so, large impacts of the death of working males have to be interpreted carefully. It is still possible that we pick up the effect of poverty on school dropouts.

One important cause of girls' decisions to drop out of school in South Africa is pregnancy. The question then arises of whether the probability of becoming pregnant during schooling is correlated with prime-age adult mortality in the household. For example, it is possible that poor families are more likely to have pregnant teenagers and face higher prime-age adult deaths than wealthy families. Again this factor was controlled for by including the value of durable goods in the household. However, it is possible for some households to have members with high biological fecundity (propensity to reproduce), which increases both the likelihood of teenage pregnancy and adult sexual activity (including extramarital sex), possibly leading to a higher incidence of HIV/AIDS-related deaths. Another potential problem arises from a positive correlation between a pregnancy shock (implying a negative shock to enrollment) and a prime-age adult mortality shock in the household. In the preceding cross-sectional analysis, data limitations make it hard to control the resulting potential downward bias. I was thus forced to set this problem aside.

Next I analyze the transition of adolescents from school to the labor force using panel data for 1998-2004. Table 5.5 shows the relationship between age in 1998 and activity in 2004—whether or not an individual is in school (employed and unemployed). Interestingly, the transition to the labor market starts above ages 12-14 in 1998. In the preliminary analysis, I used a sample aged 7-13, but it was found that children aged 7-12 (in 1998) did not contribute to the estimation owing to a very small number of transitions. Therefore—as long as enrollment is used as a measure of schooling status, as opposed to more sophisticated measures, such as attendance, grade progression, and test scores—it is not feasible to identify the transition from school to nonschool status using younger children. Therefore I focus on adolescents (defined as those aged 14-19) in this study.

Table 5.6 gives the estimation results for the conditional (fixed-effect) logit model.[17] In this analysis I ignore other activities as an endogenous choice variable since the number of observations in this group is only seven for 1998 (rendering the estimation unstable). In all specifications, I also include dummies for maternal and paternal deaths.[18]

---

[17] Unobserved fecundity is controlled as fixed effects are eliminated in the conditional logit estimation.

[18] I include parents in all ages, not restricting them to ages 15-64.

Table 5.5 Activity in 2004 by age in 1998

Age in 1998 (years)	School in 2004	Non-school in 2004	Total
6	168	1	169
7	182	1	183
8	160	2	162
9	144	4	148
10	171	6	177
11	118	8	126
12	165	25	190
13	137	60	197
14	80	58	138
15	52	76	128
16	36	69	105
17	24	104	128
18	16	93	109
19	9	103	112
20	12	98	110
21	1	85	86
22	2	112	114
23	0	114	114
24	2	99	101
25	2	104	106

Sources: University of KwaZulu-Natal / International Food Policy Research Institute / University of Wisconsin-Madison (1998, 2004).

Column 1 includes the number of deaths among prime-age (20-64) household members, maternal deaths, and paternal deaths during the period 1998-2004. First, deaths of prime-age members significantly increase adolescents' transitions from school to labor markets. Second, deaths of a mother and a father both significantly increase such transitions.

Column 2 includes the number of deaths among working prime-age household members during the period 1998-2004. Since the death of working prime-age members is a subset of prime-age deaths, we look at the additional effect that the death of working members may have. There is no additional effect on adolescents' transition from school to labor markets.

In column 3 I interact the male adolescent indicator with the above-prime-age adult mortality measures to check for gender differences in transition into the labor force. The column shows that an increase in the total number of working prime-age household members promotes a shift out of school into the labor force among adolescent males. The effect of prime-age deaths is significant without showing a gender difference. Mother's death and father's death continue to be highly significant.

Table 5.6 Impact of prime-age adult mortality on adolescent transition from school to labor market

Explanatory variable	(1)	(2)	(3)	(4)	(5)	(6)	(7)
Prime-age deaths							
(20-64 years)	2.8709	3.2951	3.4267	1.2103	0.4379		
	(4.01)	(3.29)	(3.38)	(1.34)	(0.36)		
× Male			-0.2792		1.5080		
			(1.04)		(1.25)		
Prime-age working deaths							
(20-64 years)		-1.1591	-2.3317				
		(0.76)	(1.48)				
× Male			16.712				
			(13.15)				
Prime-age deaths							
(20-44 years)				2.8765	3.0571		
				(2.87)	(3.04)		
× Male					11.493		
					(11.41)		
Male prime-age deaths							
(20-64 years)						3.6413	2.7531
						(3.54)	(2.58)
× Male							13.840
							(12.89)
Female prime-age deaths							
(20-64 years)						2.3824	2.3214
						(3.16)	(3.15)
× Male							0.1798
							(0.22)
Maternal death	16.201	16.717	16.712	15.542	15.674	15.212	15.517
	(21.14)	(21.89)	(13.15)	(21.77)	(20.47)	(20.47)	(21.06)
Paternal death	16.263	17.245	16.663	16.422	16.797	14.843	15.147
	(30.25)	(30.58)	(26.15)	(24.56)	(17.81)	(24.45)	(25.20)
Number of observations	754	754	754	754	754	754	754
Pseudo R^2	0.3358	0.3381	0.3458	0.3489	0.3536	0.3384	0.3418

Sources: University of KwaZulu-Natal / International Food Policy Research Institute / University of Wisconsin-Madison (1998, 2004).

Notes: The dependent variable equals one if the individual was in the labor force in 2004 and zero if in school. Fixed-effect logit estimation used. The numbers in parentheses are absolute z-values. Robust standard errors are used with household-level clusters. Sample consists of those aged 14-19 years in 1998.

Columns 4 and 5 add the number of prime-age deaths using the age definition 20-44 years. The results show that while the death of prime-age members using ages 20-64 is insignificant, deaths among members aged 20-44 significantly increases the transition of adolescents from school to labor markets. Interestingly, male adolescents are more likely than females to stop attending school when more economically active household members die (that is, those aged 20-44 and/or working and of prime age).

In columns 6 and 7 I decompose prime-age deaths by gender. Both male and female prime-age deaths significantly increase the transition into the labor force. The effect is slightly larger with male prime-age deaths. The death of male prime-age members has a statistically larger effect on male adolescents.

In summary, our results imply that it is more likely for male adolescents to enter the labor force when economically more active household members die—that is, males classified as of prime age (20–64), of prime age (20–44), or working and of prime age. This means that there is a substitution between male adolescents and economically active household members in their potential contribution to household income. Second, deaths of mothers and female prime-age household members affect both genders equally. This finding is consistent with the hypothesis posed earlier.

Third, in all specifications, I found that mothers' and fathers' deaths both significantly increase adolescents' entry into the labor markets. Quantitatively the impacts are much larger than that of prime-age adult deaths. The findings are largely consistent with evidence provided in the literature, but these results show that the effects of mothers' and fathers' deaths are nearly equal, while some previous studies report a larger effect of mothers' deaths.

The results in Tables 5.4 and 5.6 support the hypothesis that excess prime-age adult mortality in a society decreases the investment in human capital in the young population. I find decreased male and female schooling (increasing their entrance into the labor markets) before and after the death of prime-age adults and, more importantly, the death of parent(s).

Conclusion

My empirical results show that prime-age adult mortality has had an impact on adolescents' transition from school to labor markets and on female labor supply decisions during the period 1998–2004. This six-year period coincided with an increase in prime-age adult mortality in South Africa.

A few clear findings emerged from this research. The death of a prime-age adult in the household, parent(s), or both significantly promotes adolescent transition to the labor markets. Adolescents leave school in order to compensate for a possible loss of or reduction in household income, to smooth consumption, or to look after the household and its members. Male adolescent labor supply increases more when the death of *working* adults is anticipated in the very near future.

These results suggest that excess mortality among prime-age adult causes a reduction of human capital investments at school as well as at home. Thus the AIDS epidemic has negative effects on the formation of human capital for the next generation, not only by disrupting child schooling, as many studies have shown, but also by discouraging the continuation of schooling investment among adolescents.

Generally, in light of constrained household income owing to medical and funeral costs and limited access to formal arrangements (for example, credit) and to foster-care grants (see Meintjes et al. 2003 for South Africa), the well-being of surviving household members, including orphans, remains a challenge. As the economy confronts an increased number of young people experiencing prime-age adult mortality in their households, this challenge will need to be addressed by the South African government and the society as a whole.

CHAPTER 6

History versus Expectations

The formation of human capital in the majority population of South Africa promises the alleviation of poverty and equitable economic growth. With the burden of its apartheid legacy, the country faces enormous challenges in transforming itself into an equitable society. Given the political difficulty of redistributing assets from the historically advantaged minority to the disadvantaged majority, the formation of human capital in the latter group can be a long-term solution to these challenges, as it builds new assets the poor can own and direct. However, the transformation of a society through the broad-based formation of human capital, especially among Africans, requires a relatively long time span.

This monograph delivers two basic messages. First, though education is at the center of human capital formation, the dynamic aspects of human capital formation in individuals call for a wider perspective. Part 2 demonstrated that human capital formation is dynamic in the sense that it starts in early childhood—even before childbirth. Malnutrition during early childhood owing to poverty reduces achievements at the schooling stage. Policy interventions aimed at enhancing healthy child growth (such as the current child support grants) are needed to guarantee the outcomes expected from the government's effort to develop public school education. In South Africa the HIV/AIDS epidemic adversely affects schooling progress among adolescents, increasing their entry into the labor markets. Therefore, it is important to support households that are vulnerable to adverse shocks and protect children from the negative impacts of such shocks.

Second, as Part 1 showed, access to opportunities is still unequal across different segments of the society. Given the historical path the country has taken, it is important to guarantee equal opportunities for the formation of human capital to the African majority. In particular, relaxing financial constraints in formerly African schools and households is an urgent priority.

Chapter 1 posed two questions regarding returns to schooling in South Africa: Why do returns to schooling differ across population groups? And why do those returns show convexity—low returns up to high school, with significantly positive returns at the completion of high school or at higher levels?

It appears to me that an answer to the first question is related to differences in the quality of education available to different groups of the society. Part 1 showed that local resource constraints, reflected in school fees, potentially limit the quality of education available in certain communities, though I also confirmed that government subsidies had relaxed those constraints. In this sense, it is interesting to observe that recent returns to schooling have been higher among the Indian/Asian population than among others. The labor markets still demonstrate whites' advantage in accessing jobs with higher wages.

The convexity question also seems to be related to the quality of education as well as the high unemployment rate in the South African labor markets. It is possible that labor demands that are biased in favor of a skilled labor force create rigidity in the demand-supply mismatch, concentrating unemployment among the less educated. The relatively low pass rate in matriculation at grade 12 exacerbates this problem.

As our finding in Chapter 3 suggests, however, the progressive allocation of government budgets to schools, supported by the Norms and Standards for School Funding, is expected to improve the situation faced by historically disadvantaged schools and communities.

Appendix

Model for Chapters 2 and 3

I set up a simple static model of school finance and the demand for educators to confirm intuitions regarding the roles of liquidity constraints, government subsidy, and government coordination in the determination of LERs. Suppose there are a finite number of public schools under a government, and that each school maximizes the per-learner output from education, given its budget constraint, without government intervention. Assume that each school can employ educators freely and that the number of learners changes exogenously at each school, for example, owing to migration and population growth.

Each school has a target LER in each period that maximizes the efficiency in education production, $y_{it} = y^* + \xi_{it}$, where ξ_{it} is independent and identically distributed with zero mean and finite variance. We assume that y^* is small enough, and we ignore a negative range of y_{it}.[1] ξ_{it} could reflect transitory changes in school environments.

Let $e_i(L_i, H_i)$ denote an efficienty function, where L_i and H_i are learners and educators in school i, respectively. I assume the efficiency function takes a quadratic loss form: $e_i(L_i, H_i) = \left[1 - (y_{it} - \frac{L_i}{H_i})^2\right]$, where LER determines the learning efficiency.[2] The total educational outcome is defined as $e_i(L_i, H_i)L_i$. Each school has its static budget constraint, $q_iL_i + G_iwH_i$, where q_i is the school fee, G_i is a subsidy from the government, w is the wage rate (exogenous) for educators, and $H_i = H_i^s + H_i^u$ for two types of educators, subsidized and nonsubsidized, H_i^s and H_i^u, respectively. By definition, the budget constraint can be separated into two constraints: a government subsidy constraint, $G_i \geq wH_i$, and a school fee constraint, $q_iL_i \geq wH_i^u$. Nonsubsidized teachers are paid only from school fees. However, since the quality of subsidized and nonsubsidized

[1] The optimal level of LER can change as endowment for and technology deployment in education production vary across schools, if these factors alter the marginal productivity of educators. When other nonpersonnel inputs and LERs are substitutable, equal LERs are not necessary for equal education output.

[2] In the range of LERs below the target, the efficiency is increasing in LER. It is assumed that with positive externalities among peer learners, an increase in number of learners raises the efficiency. However, if this effect is negligible, the target level can be set arbitrarily small.

educators is the same in this framework, the two budget constraints can be added together. Assume that the government decides the per-learner amount of subsidy, g_i, so $G_i = g_i L_i$ and $g_i \geq 0$ for all i (the government does not impose a tax).

The school fee is bounded by some limit, $\overline{q_i}\,(f)$, determined by the socio-economic circumstances, f, of the school. In particular, the fee is determined by income level and distribution.[3] In fact, school fees are determined by SGBs consisting of educators and community leaders, such that most parents can afford to pay them. Unless the government subsidy g_i offsets $q_i(f)$, local condition f affects $\frac{L}{H}$.

School maximizes the per-learner education output subject to the budget constraint:

$$\max_{x,q} E_t e_i(L_i, H_i) = \left[1 - (y_{it} - \frac{L_i}{H_i})^2\right]$$

s.t.

$$G_i \geq wH_i^s$$

$$q_i L_i \geq wH_i^u.$$

Rearranging the budget constraint, we define $\phi(q_i(f); w, g_i)$:

$$\phi(q_i; w, g_i) \equiv \frac{w}{q_i(f) + g_i} \leq \frac{L_i}{H_i}. \tag{A.1}$$

The LER is constrained below by the ratio of educator wage (per-educator cost) to the sum of the school fee and the per-learner subsidy (per-learner revenue). When the school decides on the school fee and employs educators, the determination of the school fee is simple: $q_i^*(f) = q_i(f)$, that is, collect the highest school fees.[4] In this model I assume that, at least in the short

[3] For example, if community members vote for a school fee, we predict that the fee will be determined by the median community income.

[4] Since 1996 school fees for public schools have been determined by the SGB, which consists of the principal, educators, parents (including community leaders), and sometimes learners at the secondary level. Therefore, the level of the school fee reflects opinions within the community. In community-school governance, the school fee increases as the median of monthly household income increases and as the standard deviation of monthly household income decreases. The former result is consistent with the voting implication, while the latter implies that school fee determination is anti-inequality. In this sense, school governance is altruistic to poor families who have difficulty in paying school fees, but it potentially sacrifices school quality (Yamauchi and Nishiyama 2005).

run, the number of learners does not change immediately in response to an increase in school fees (that is, inelastic enrollment), but also that the fees are determined such that most parents can afford to pay them.[5]

Suppose now that budget constraints are not binding. Then the optimal solution is

$$x_i^* \equiv \frac{L_i}{H_i^*} = y^* > \phi(\bar{q}_i(f),\, g_i;\, w).$$

In this case $H_i = \beta^* L_i$, where $\beta^* = \frac{1}{y^*}$. Next consider the case in which the budget constraint is binding: $y^* < \phi(\bar{q}_i(f),\, g_i;\, w)$. In this case:

$$\begin{aligned} H_i &= \frac{1}{\phi \bar{q}_i(f),\, g_i;\, w)} L_i \\ &= \beta^* L_i + \left[\frac{1}{\phi(\bar{q}_i(f),\, g_i;\, w)} - \beta^*\right] L_i \qquad \text{(A.2)} \\ &= \beta^* L_i + \left[\frac{w}{\bar{q}_i(f) + g_i} - \beta^*\right] L_i, \end{aligned}$$

where $w < \beta^*(\bar{q}_i(f) + g_i)$. The second term is an efficiency loss in terms of the number of educators. The government will allocate the subsidies to those with binding budget constraints. Next consider the government's allocation of school subsidies. Assume that the government maximizes the total educational output $\sum_i e_i l_i$ subject to its budget constraint but does not allocate any subsidy to those schools that are able to attain optimal ratios:

$$\max_{\{g_i\}_i} \sum_{i \mid y^* < \phi(\bar{q}i,0;w)} \left[1 - (y^* - \frac{w}{q_i(f) + g_i})^2\right] L_i$$

s.t.

$$\sum_{i \mid y^* < \phi(\bar{q}i,0;w)} g_i L_i \leq G.$$

[5] Yamauchi and Nishiyama (2005) show that the proportion of learners who cannot pay school fees, including both those who postpone payment and those who receive official exemptions, is positively correlated with the level of the school fees. The result, however, does not directly show the school drop-out rate. My interviews with school principals indicate that those parents

Without the government budget constratint, the necessary condition is $g_i^* = wy^* - \overline{q_i}(f)$. In general we have $2[y^* - \phi_i(g_i)][-\phi'(g_i)] = \lambda$, where λ is the Lagrangian multiplier. From this we also know that when $\overline{q_i}(f)$ decreases, g_i increases to compensate for gaps in the capability of collecting school fees (community endowment). In other words, LERs are equalized under the benevolent government's unitary decision.

So, without government intervention, LERs are determined by school-level liquidity (budget) constraints, provided that the best ratio is identical in all schools no matter to which racial group they belong. However, we expect that with active government interventions, the ratios will be equalized across all schools. In particular, the subsidy is allocated more to those schools in less favorable socioeconomic circumstances, that is, those with larger initial LERs.

The 1998 Norms and Standards for School Funding

Sections that are relevant to this monograph are the following:

> 45. The SASA [South African School Act] imposes a responsibility on all public school governing bodies to do their utmost to improve the quality of education in their schools by raising additional resources to supplement those which the state provides from public funds (section 36). All parents, but particularly those who are less poor or who have good incomes, are thereby encouraged to increase their own direct financial and other contributions to the quality of their children's education in public schools. The act does not interfere unreasonably with parents' discretion under the law as to how to spend their own resources on their children's education.
>
> 46. Ironically, given the emphasis on redress and equity, the funding provisions of the Act appear to have worked thus far to the advantage of public schools patronized by middle-class and wealthy parents. The apartheid regime favored such communities with high-quality facilities, equipment and resources. Vigorous fund-raising by parent bodies, including commercial sponsorships and fee income, have enabled many such schools to add to their facilities, equipment and learning resources, and expand their range of cultural and sporting activities. Since 1995, when such schools have been required to down-size their

who cannot pay school fees are often required to provide services to the schools, such as cleaning the school facilities, but there is no systematic evidence suggesting that this is the norm in the country.

In the empirical analysis, since we look only at the relationship between changes in number of learners and educators, we do not directly examine the effect of school fees.

staff establishments, many have been able to recruit additional staff on governing body contracts, paid from the school fund.

47. Poor people, on the other hand, especially in former homeland areas, have contributed a disproportionate share of their incomes over many decades to their building, upkeep and improvement of schools, through school funds and other contributions, including physical labor. All too many schools in poor rural and urban working-class communities still suffer the legacy of large classes, deplorable physical conditions, and absence of learning resources, despite a major RDP National School Building Programme, and many other projects paid directly from provincial budgets. Yet the educators and learners in poor schools are expected to achieve the same levels of learning and teaching as their compatriots.

48. Such contractions within the same public school system reflect past discriminatory investment in schooling, and vast current disparities in the personal income of parents. The present document addresses these inequalities by establishing a sharply progressive state funding policy for ordinary public schools, which favors poor communities.

Model for Chapter 4

This section introduces a simple model in which parents decide how much to invest in child health and schooling, resulting in returns in the labor market. For simplicity, we treat the age distribution of children as exogenous and assume that children enter the labor market in the final stage. Health is formed in the first stage, while schooling investment is undertaken in the next stage.[6]

In the pre-primary-school stage, per capita consumption determines health capital h_j for child j, $h_j = f(c_1, x) + \varepsilon_{j1}$, where c_1 is per capita consumption in the household; x is predetermined community and household characteristics, such as the availability of healthcare facilities and personnel and parents' schooling; and ε_{j1} is an idiosyncratic health shock. For simplicity, health capital accumulates only until age a^*, when a child enters the schooling stage. The investment component $f(c_1, x)$ is characterized by the properties $\frac{\partial f}{\partial c_1} > 0$ and $\frac{\partial^2 f}{\partial c_1 \partial x} > 0$. For simplicity, I assume that $c_1 = y$. Given that h is child height, c is specifically intended to capture nutritional intake.

[6] Nutrition intakes until the age of 3 are regarded as very important in forming child health capital, measured by height-for-age z-score. Although weight-for-age z-score fluctuates over time (age) owing to changes in nutrition intakes (that is, consumption), height-for-age z-score is less likely to change after the age of 3. In the context of dynamic human capital production, therefore, child health is measured by the height-for-age z-score.

At the second stage, knowledge capital k_j accumulates with schooling investments s_j. The knowledge production function is given as

$$k_j = g(s_j, h_j, x) + \varepsilon_{j2},$$

where investment $g(s_{j2}, h_j, x)$ has health capital as its argument. Complementarity between schooling and health investments is captured by $\frac{\partial^2 g}{\partial s \partial h} > 0$. An implication of such complementarity (or substitutability) is that parents want to observe the outcome of health capital among their children in order to optimally decide schooling investments in the children. Owing to the sequential nature of human capital investment, parents can learn about the total outcomes of child human capital and their labor-market returns from the outcomes of early-stage nutrition and health investments.[7]

The household budget constraint in the second stage is

$$c_2 + p\sum_j s_j = y + \sum_j w(h_j)[T - s_j] + b,$$

where $w(h_j)$ is the opportunity cost of schooling (returns to health capital), T is the time endowment for the child, p is the school fee, b is savings and loans, and y is exogenous household income. It is assumed that the opportunity costs increase with health capital, that is, $w'(h) \geq 0$.[8] Assume that the child cannot work at the pre-primary-school stage, and can work in the labor market only when he or she enters school.[9]

---

[7] Cunha et al. (2004) summarize some key concepts in the sequential development of child human capital. They focus on cognitive and noncognitive development. Their analysis does not directly include health and nutritional status as part of human capital in child development. The exclusion of health capital from the analysis results in a framework in which they can focus on human capital production function and the complementarity and substitutability of different inputs (for example, at the early-childhood and schooling stages). In this appendix, children are also considered as working in the labor market or participating in other activities where health capital has economic returns. This institutional setting creates implications that offset the health-schooling complementarity effect.

[8] It is also important to note that the income opportunity in the child wage $w(h)$ is not necessarily related to labor markets. It may also capture activities such as child care and self-employment.

[9] Several qualifications follow. First, I assume that income from siblings, parents, and credit is pooled in the household budget constraint and is therefore perfectly substitutable. Second, to describe the income process, the model does not assume a production function in which adult and child members supply labor inputs that are not perfectly substitutable. This assumption is suitable in our empirical setting of South Africa, where wage employment (including formal and informal jobs) is a major source of income. Third, the utility function does not include leisure, which is imperfectly substitutable between household members (for example, Pitt and Rosenzweig 1990).

Parents maximize the objective function

$$\max_{s_j, b} u(c_2) + \beta E \sum_j V(W(k_j, h_j) - (1 + r)b_j),$$

which captures the discounted sum of expected utilities from consumption over time and the final-period returns from children. Discount factor β has an interpretation of altruism to children, who have an increasing and concave utility function V. Assume that $W(k_j, h) = R_k k_j + R_h h_j$, where R_k and R_h are financial returns to knowledge and health capital, respectively. In this version, since we do not have uncertainty in the future returns to human capital, we omit the expectations operator. If the wage function is strictly concave, parents have incentives to equalize human capital among their children.

The first-order conditions at the second stage are

$$\lambda^* = u'(c_2^*) = \beta(1 + r)V'(c^j)$$

$$\{w(h_j) + p\} u'(c_2^*) = \beta V'(c^j) \frac{\partial g}{\partial s_j} (s_j, h_j, x) R_k',$$

where λ^* denotes the Lagrange multiplier associated with the stage 2 budget constraint. These conditions provide the schooling function $k^*(y, h_j, x)$. At the first stage, the problem is trivial, since exogenous income and shocks determine investment in health capital. Therefore, with a perfect loan market, the effect of health on schooling depends on

$$\frac{\partial s_j^*}{\partial h_j} > 0 \Leftrightarrow \frac{\partial^2 g(s_j, h_j)}{\partial s_j \partial h_j} R_k > w'(h_j)(1 + r).$$

Preference and household income do not enter the condition. In this case, parents compare returns and opportunity costs for schooling. The important point is that child health capital can alter both returns and costs. If the opportunity cost does not increase with health capital (that is, $w'(h) = 0$), an increase in health capital will raise the optimal level of schooling if health and knowledge capital are complementary.

In short, better health increases schooling, but it may also increase the probability that children are taken out of school to work either at home or in the market.

Next consider the case in which $b = 0$, where credit opportunity is closed. Given the second-order condition, the effect of h_j on s_j depends on

$$\beta \frac{\partial^2 g}{\partial s_j \partial h_j} R_k V'(c^j) + \beta V''(c^j) R_k \frac{\partial g}{\partial s_j} \left\{ R_k \frac{\partial g}{\partial h_j} + R_h \right\}$$

$$\gtreqless w'(h_j)u'(c_2^*) + \{w(h_j) + p\} \frac{\partial u'(c_2^*)}{\partial h_j}.$$

There are four effects in this condition. First, the complementarity effect is summarized in the first term on the left-hand side, which increases schooling investment. Second, the concavity of the child utility function (that is, $V''(c^j) < 0$) creates incentives to equalize the human capital outcomes and the future returns, which decreases schooling investment for children with greater health capital (the second term on the left-hand side). Parents are averse to sibling inequality. Third, an increase in health capital augments income opportunity outside school, which increases the opportunity cost of schooling investment (the first term on the right-hand side). Fourth, an increase in health capital also relaxes the household budget constraint, which weakens the necessity to work outside and increases schooling investment (the second term on the right-hand side). Whether or not health capital increases schooling investment depends on the magnitudes of these factors.

It is easy to see the effect of other siblings' health capital on schooling. In this case, we only have the budget-relaxing effect, and an increase of other siblings' health capital always relaxes the household budget constraint, which increases schooling investment.[10] Interestingly, however, the effect of other siblings' health capital on schooling investment exists only when the financial market is imperfect. An exogenous improvement in other siblings' health relaxes the budget constraint, which reduces the marginal utility λ^*. If liquidity constraint is more likely to bind as the household income drops, the sibling effect is more likely to hold among poor households. This does not happen when the loan market is perfect.

We have two other conjectures. First, in the case of the convex return function R_k, for which the second-order condition does not always hold, we expect some corner solutions. Parents can maximize welfare by investing in some children while ignoring others. When health capital is complementary to schooling investment, parents concentrate schooling investments in well-endowed children, if the labor market wage is constant. However, greater health capital also raises opportunity costs, which decreases schooling invest-

[10] See Parrish and Willis (1993) for related evidence. See also Black, Devereux, and Salvanes (2005) for birth-order effects on child education.

ments. If the latter effect is sufficiently small, we expect that schooling inequality between siblings will diverge.[11]

Second, suppose that children are born in different time periods. In the case of a small discount factor, parents may want to invest more in the schooling of older siblings, sacrificing the human capital for younger siblings, in order to gain returns to human capital as early as possible. If older siblings' time input is important (included) in young siblings' health capital production, older siblings can work at home to take care of younger siblings. In this case there is a trade-off between schooling investments in older siblings and time input in the health capital formation of younger siblings, which depends on the discount factor.[12]

---

[11] Quisumbing, Estudillo, and Otsuka (2003) present evidence from the rural Philippines, where boys are likely to inherit land, showing that parents invest more in the schooling of daughters than in that of sons, to equalize lifetime earnings between them. In the Philippines Schady (2003) and Yamauchi (2005a) both show that the schooling return function is convex; the latter contrasts this finding to the case of Thailand, where schooling returns are concave.

[12] Nonneutrality of birth order and sibling's sex composition in child human capital investment are pointed out and analyzed in, for example, Rosenzweig (1986), Butcher and Case (1994), Rosenzweig and Wolpin (2000), and Black, Devereux, and Salvanes (2005).

References

Actuarial Society of South Africa. 2002. ASSA2002 AIDS and demographic model. <http://aids.actuarialsociety.org.za/ASSA2002-3157.htm>. Accessed September 22, 2010.

Ainsworth, M., and D. Filmer. 2006. Inequalities in children's schooling: AIDS, orphanhood, poverty and gender. *World Development* 34 (6): 1099–1128.

Ainsworth, M., K. Beegle, and G. Koda. 2005. The impact of adult mortality and parental deaths on primary schooling in north-western Tanzania. *Journal of Development Studies* 41 (3): 412–439.

Alderman, H., J. Behrman, V. Lavy, and R. Menon. 2000. Child health and school enrollment: A longitudinal analysis. *Journal of Human Resources* 36 (1): 185–205.

Alderman, H., J. Hoddinott, and B. Kinsey. 2006. Long term consequences of early childhood malnutrition. *Oxford Economic Papers* 58 (3): 450–474.

Anderson, K., A. Case, and D. Lam. 2001. Causes and consequences of schooling outcomes in South Africa: Evidence from survey data. *Social Dynamics* 27 (1): 37–59.

Angrist, J., and V. Lavy. 1999. Using Maimonides' rule to estimate the effect of class size on scholastic achievement. *Quarterly Journal of Economics* 114 (2): 533–575.

Ardington, C., and M. Leibbrandt. 2010. Orphanhood and schooling in South Africa: Trends in the vulnerability of orphans between 1993 and 2005. *Economic Development and Cultural Change* 58 (3): 507–537.

Becker, G. 1962. Investment in human capital: A theoretical analysis. *Journal of Political Economy* 70 (5): 9–49.

Beegle, K. 2005. Labor effects of adult mortality in Tanzanian households. *Economic Development and Cultural Change* 53 (3): 655–683.

Beegle, K., J. De Weerdt, and S. Dercon. 2006. Orphanhood and the long-run impact on children. *American Journal of Agricultural Economics* 88 (5): 1266–1272.

Behrman, J. R., H. Alderman, and J. Hoddinott. 2004. Hunger and malnutrition. In *Global crisis, global solutions*, ed. B. Lomborg. Cambridge, Mass., U.S.A.: Cambridge University Press.

Behrman, J. R., J. Hoddinott, J. A. Maluccio, E. Soler-Hampejsek, E. L. Behrman, R. Martorell, M. Ramirez-Zea, and A. D. Steind. 2006. What determines adult cognitive skills? Impacts of pre-schooling, schooling and post-schooling experiences in Guatemala. International Food Policy Research Institute, Washington, D.C. Manuscript.

Bennell, P. 2005. The impact of the AIDS epidemic on the schooling of orphans and other directly affected children in Sub-Saharan Africa. *Journal of Development Studies* 41 (3): 467–488.

Bhorat, H., M. Leibbrandt, M. Maziya, S. Van der Berga, and I. Woolard. 2001. *Fighting poverty: Labour markets and inequality in South Africa.* Cape Town, South Africa: University of Cape Town Press.

Black, S. E., P. J. Devereux, and K. G. Salvanes. 2005. The more the merrier? The effect of family size and birth order on children's education. *Quarterly Journal of Economics* 120 (2): 669–700.

——. 2007. From the cradle to the labor market? The effect of birth weight on adult outcomes. *Quarterly Journal of Economics* 122 (1): 409–439.

Bloch, G., L. Chisholm, B. Fleisch, and M. Mabizela, eds. 2008. *Investment choices in South African education*. Johannesburg, South Africa: Wits University Press.

Bot, M., D. Wilson, and S. Dove. 2000. *Education atlas of South Africa*. Durban, South Africa: EduAction.

Butcher, K., and A. Case. 1994. The effect of sibling sex composition on women's education and earnings. *Quarterly Journal of Economics* 109 (3): 531–563.

Card, D. 2001. Estimating the return to schooling: Progress in some persistent econometric problems. *Econometrica* 69 (5): 1127–1160.

Card, D., and A. Krueger. 1996. *Labor market effects of school quality: Theory and evidence*. NBER Working Paper 5450. Cambridge, Mass., U.S.A.: National Bureau of Economic Research.

Case, A., and C. Ardington. 2006. The impact of parental death on school enrollment and achievement: Longitudinal evidence from South Africa. *Demography* 43 (3): 401–420.

Case, A., and A. Deaton. 1999. School inputs and educational outcomes in South Africa. *Quarterly Journal of Economics* 114 (3): 1047–1084.

Case, A., and M. Yogo. 1999. *Does school quality matter? Returns to education and the characteristics of schools in South Africa*. NBER Working Paper 7399. Cambridge, Mass., U.S.A.: National Bureau of Economic Research.

Case, A., C. Paxson, and J. Ableidinger. 2004. Orphans in Africa: Parental death, poverty, and school enrollment. *Demography* 41 (3): 483–508.

Chamberlain, G. 1984. Panel data. In *Handbook of econometrics*, Vol. 2, ed. Z. Griliches and M. D. Intriligator. Amsterdam: North-Holland.

Chattopadhyay, R., and E. Duflo. 2004. Women as policy makers: Evidence from an India-wide randomized policy experiment in India. *Econometrica* 72 (5): 1409–1443.

Crouch, L. 1996. Public education equity and efficiency in South Africa: Lessons for other countries. *Economics of Education Review* 15 (2): 125–137.

Cunha, F., J. Heckman, L. Lochner, and D. Masterov. 2004. Interpreting the evidence on life cycle skill formation. University of Chicago. Manuscript.

Department of Education. 2002. *Report on the School Register of Needs 2000 survey*. Pretoria, South Africa.

Dieden, S. 2004. Integration into the South African core economy: Household-level covariates. *Development Southern Africa* 21 (1): 33–57.

Donovan, C., L. Bailey, E. Mpyisi, and M. Weber. 2003. *Prime-age adult morbidity and mortality in rural Rwanda: Effects on household income, agricultural production, and food security strategies*. Research Report. Pretoria, South Africa: Food Security Research Project and Division of Agricultural Statistics, Ministry of Agriculture, Livestock and Forestry.

Dorrington, R., L. Johnson, D. Bradshaw, and D. Timothy-John. 2006. The demographic impact of HIV/AIDS in South Africa. Centre for Actuarial Research, South African Medical Research Council and Actuarial Society of South Africa, Cape Town. Manuscript.

Dustman, C., N. Rajah, and V. Soest. 2003. Class size, education, and wages. *Economic Journal* 113 (2): F99–F120.

EduAction. 2001. *Technical report: School Register of Needs 2000 survey*. Durban.

Epstein, B. 2004. The demographic impact of HIV/AIDS. In *The macroeconomics of HIV/AIDS*, ed. M. Haacker. Washington, D.C.: International Monetary Fund.

Evans, D., and E. Miguel. 2007. Orphans and schooling in Africa: A longitudinal analysis. *Demography* 44 (1): 35–57.

Fitzgerald, J., P. Gottschalk, and R. Moffitt. 1998a. An analysis of sample attrition in panel data: The Michigan Panel Study of Income Dynamics. *Journal of Human Resources* 33 (2): 251–299.

——. 1998b. The impact of attrition in the panel study of income dynamics on intergenerational analysis. *Journal of Human Resources* 33 (2): 300–344.

Fleisch, B. 2008. *Primary education in crisis: Why South African schoolchildren underachieve in reading and mathematics*. Cape Town, South Africa: Juta.

Foster, A. 1995. Prices, credit markets and child growth in low-income rural areas. *Economic Journal* 105 (430): 551–570.

Foster, A. D., and M. R. Rosenzweig. 2001. Democratization, decentralization, and the distribution of local public goods in a poor rural economy. Brown University, Providence, R.I., U.S.A. Mimeograph.

Glewwe, P., H. Jacoby, and E. King. 2001. The impact of early childhood nutritional status on cognitive development: Does the timing of malnutrition matter? *Journal of Public Economics* 81 (3): 345–368.

Groenewald, P., N. Nannan, D. Bourne, R. Laubscher, and D. Bradshaw. 2005. Identifying deaths from AIDS in South Africa. *AIDS* 19 (2): 194–201.

Haddad, L., and H. Bouis. 1991. The impact of nutritional status on agricultural productivity: Wage evidence from the Philippines. *Oxford Bulletin of Economics and Statistics* 53 (1): 45–68.

Hallman, K. 2004. *Socioeconomic disadvantage and unsafe sexual behaviors among young women and men in South Africa*. Policy Research Division Working Paper 190. New York: Population Council.

Hanushek, E. 1998. Conclusions and controversies about the effectiveness of school resources. *Federal Reserve Board of New York Economic Policy Review* 4 (1): 11–27.

Hayami, Y., and Y. Godo. 2005. *Development economics: From the poverty to the wealth of nations*. Oxford: Oxford University Press.

Hoddinott, J., and B. Kinsey. 2001. Child growth in the time of drought. *Oxford Bulletin of Economics and Statistics* 63 (4): 409–436.

Hoxby, C. 2000. The effects of class size on student achievement: New evidence from natural population variation. *Quarterly Journal of Economics* 116 (4): 1239–1286.

Kingdon, G., and J. Knight. 2006. The measurement of unemployment when unemployment is high. *Labour Economics* 13 (3): 291–315.

Kriege, D., S. Cairns, B. Makalima, and D. Scott. 1994. *Education atlas of South Africa.* Durban, South Africa: Education Foundation.

Krueger, A. 1999. Experimental estimates of educational production functions. *Quarterly Journal of Economics* 114 (2): 497–532.

KwaZulu-Natal, Department of Education. Various years. Norms and standards database. Pietermaritzburg, South Africa. Database.

Lam, D., C. Ardington, and M. Leibbrandt. 2009. Schooling as a lottery: Racial differences in school advancement in urban South Africa. University of Michigan, Ann Arbor. Manuscript.

Lazear, E. P. 2001. Educational production. *Quarterly Journal of Economics* 116 (3): 777–804.

Lucas, R. E., Jr. 1988. On the mechanics of economic development. *Journal of Monetary Economics* 22 (1): 3–42.

Maluccio, J. A., J. Hoddinott, J.R. Behrman, A. Quisumbing, R. Martorell, and A.D. Stein. 2009. The impact of an experimental nutritional intervention on education into adulthood in rural Guatemala. *Economic Journal* 119 (537): 734–763.

Marais, M. 1995. The distribution of resources in education in South Africa. *Economics of Education Review* 14(1): 47–52.

May, J., J. Agüero, M. Carter, and I. Timaeus. 2007. The KwaZulu-Natal Income Dynamics Study (KIDS) third wave: Methods, first findings and an agenda for future research. *Development Southern Africa* 24 (5): 629–648.

Meintjes, H., D. Budlender, S. Giese, and L. Johnson. 2003. Children in "need of care" or in need of cash? Questioning social security provisions for orphans in the context of the South African AIDS pandemic. Children's Institute and Centre for Actuarial Research, Cape Town, South Africa. Manuscript.

Munshi, K., and J. Myaux. 2002. Development as a process of social change: An application to the fertility transition. Brown University, Providence, R.I., U.S.A. Manuscript.

Oster, E. 2005. Sexually transmitted infections, sexual behavior, and HIV/AIDS epidemic. *Quarterly Journal of Economics* 102 (2): 467–515.

Parrish, W. L., and R. J. Willis. 1993. Daughters, education and family budgets: Taiwan experiences. *Journal of Human Resources* 28 (4): 863–898.

Pitt, M., and M. R. Rosenzweig. 1990. Estimating the intrahousehold incidence of illness: Child health and gender inequality in the allocation of time. *International Economic Review* 31 (4): 969–980.

Quisumbing, A., J. Estudillo, and K. Otsuka. 2003. *Land and schooling: Transferring wealth across generations.* Baltimore, Md., U.S.A.: Johns Hopkins University Press for the International Food Policy Research Institute.

Republic of South Africa. 1996a. *National education policy act.* Pretoria, South Africa.

———. 1996b. *South African school act.* Pretoria, South Africa.

———. 1998. *National norms and standards for school funding.* Pretoria, South Africa: National Department of Education.

Republic of South Africa, Department of Education. 1996. School register of needs 1996. Pretoria, South Africa. Database.

——. 2000. School register of needs 2000. Pretoria, South Africa. Database.

——. 2002. Annual school survey 2002. Pretoria, South Africa. Database.

Republic of South Africa, Statistics South Africa. 2001. Census 2001 community profile database. Pretoria, South Africa. Database.

——. 2003. Labor force survey, September 2003. Pietermaritzburg, South Africa. CD-ROM.

Romer, P. M. 1986. Increasing returns and the long-run growth. *Journal of Political Economy* 94 (5): 1002-1037.

Rosenzweig, M. R. 1986. Birth spacing and sibling inequality: Asymmetric information within the family. *International Economic Review* 27 (1): 55-76.

Rosenzweig, M. R., and K. I. Wolpin. 2000. Natural "natural experiments" in economics. *Journal of Economic Literature* 38 (4): 827-874

Schady, N. 2003. Convexity and sheepskin effects in the human capital earnings function: Recent evidence from Filipino men. *Oxford Bulletin of Economics and Statistics* 65 (2): 171-196.

Schultz, T. W. 1961. Investment in human capital. *American Economic Review* 51 (1): 1-17.

——. 1975. The ability to deal with disequilibria. *Journal of Economic Literature* 13 (3): 827-846.

Selod, H., and Y. Zenou. 2003. Private versus public schools in post-apartheid South African cities: Theory and policy implications. *Journal of Development Economics* 71 (2): 351-394.

Shindler, J., and B. Fleisch. 2007. Schooling for all in South Africa: Closing the gap. *International Review of Education* 53 (2): 135-157.

Smith, J. 2005. *The impact of childhood health on adult labor market outcomes.* Working Paper 319. Santa Monica, Calif., U.S.A.: RAND Corporation.

South African Labour and Development Research Unit, University of Cape Town. 1994. Project for statistics on living standards and development: South Africans rich and poor—Baseline household statistics. Cape Town, South Africa.

Statistics South Africa. 2005. *Mortality and causes of death in South Africa, 2005: Findings from death notification.* Statistical Release P0309.3. Pretoria, South Africa.

Steele, F., A. Vignoles, and A. Jenkins. 2007. The effect of school resources on pupil attainment: A multilevel simultaneous equation modeling approach. *Journal of the Royal Statistical Society: Series A (Statistics in Society)* 170 (3): 801-824.

Strauss, J. 1986. Does better nutrition raise farm productivity? *Journal of Political Economy* 94 (2): 297-320.

Strauss, J., and D. Thomas. 1995. Human resources: Empirical modeling of household and family decisions. In *Handbook of development economics,* Vol. 3, ed. J. R. Behrman and T. N. Srinivasan. Amsterdam, Netherlands: Elsevier.

Thomas, D., and J. Strauss. 1997. Health and wages: Evidence on men and women in urban Brazil. *Journal of Econometrics* 77 (1): 159-185.

Thomas, D., E. Frankenberg, and J. Smith. 2001. Lost but not forgotten: Attrition and follow-up in the Indonesia Family Life Survey. *Journal of Human Resources* 36 (3): 556-592.

Timaeus, I., and M. Jasseh. 2004. Adult mortality in Sub-Saharan Africa: Evidence from demographic and heath surveys. *Demography* 41 (4): 757-772.

Ueyama, M., and F. Yamauchi. 2009. Marriage behavior response to AIDS mortality: Evidence from Malawi. *Demography* 46 (1): 43-63.

University of KwaZulu-Natal / International Food Policy Research Institute / University of Wisconsin-Madison. 1998. KwaZulu-Natal Income Dynamics Study 2 (KIDS-2), 1998. http://www.ifpri.org/dataset/south-africa-kwazulu-natal-income-dynamics-study-kids-1993-1998. Accessed September 22, 2010.

——. 2004. KwaZulu-Natal Income Dynamics Study 3 (KIDS-3). http://sds.ukzn.ac.za/default.php?11,0,0,0,0. Accessed September 22, 2010.

Van der Berg, S. 2007. Apartheid's enduring legacy: Inequalities in education. *Journal of African Economies* 16 (5): 849-880.

Wobst, P., and C. Arndt. 2004. HIV/AIDS and labor force upgrading in Tanzania. *World Development* 32 (11): 1831-1847.

World Bank. 1993. *The East Asian miracle: Economic growth and public policy*. Washington, D.C.

Yamano, T., and T. Jayne. 2005. Working-age adult mortality and primary school attendance in rural Kenya. *Economic Development and Cultural Change* 53 (3): 619-653.

Yamauchi, F. 2003. Early transition from school to market: Labor market consequences of grade repetition in South Africa. International Food Policy Research Institute, Washington D.C. Mimeograph.

——. 2005a. Why do schooling returns differ? Screening, private schools and labor markets in the Philippines and Thailand. *Economic Development and Cultural Change* 53 (4): 959-981.

——. 2005b. Race, equity, and public schools in post-apartheid South Africa: Equal opportunity for all kids? *Economics of Education Review* 24 (2): 213-233.

——. 2006. Convergence over space and generations in the post-apartheid South Africa. *Hosei University Economic Review* 73 (4): 39-68.

——. 2007a. Social learning, neighborhood effects and investment in human capital: Evidence from green revolution India. *Journal of Development Economics* 83 (1): 37-62.

——. 2007b. *Marriage, schooling and excess mortality among prime-age adults: Evidence from South Africa*. IFPRI Discussion Paper 691. Washington, D.C.: International Food Policy Research Institute.

——. 2008. Early childhood nutrition, schooling and sibling inequality in a dynamic context: Evidence from South Africa. *Economic Development and Cultural Change* 56 (3): 657-682.

——. 2010. School quality, clustering and government subsidy in post-apartheid South Africa. *Economics of Education Review*, forthcoming. DOI: 10.1016/j.econedurev.2010.08.002. Accessed September 8, 2010.

Yamauchi, F., and S. Nishiyama. 2005. *Community, inequality and local public goods: Evidence from school financing in South Africa*. FCND Discussion Paper 201. Washington, D.C.: International Food Policy Research Institute.

Yamauchi, F., T. Buthelezi, and M. Velia. 2008. Impacts of prime-age adult mortality on labour supply: Evidence from adolescents and women in South Africa. *Oxford Bulletin of Economics and Statistics* 70 (3): 375–398.

Young, A. 2005. The gift of the dying: The tragedy of AIDS and the welfare of future African generations. *Quarterly Journal of Economics* 120 (2): 423–466.

Zimmerman, F. 2003. Cinderella goes to school: The effects of child fostering on school enrollment in South Africa. *Journal of Human Resources* 38 (3): 557–590.

About the Author

Futoshi Yamauchi is a senior research fellow in the Poverty, Health, and Nutrition Division of the International Food Policy Research Institute, Washington, D.C.

Index

Page numbers for entries occurring in figures are suffixed by *f*, those for entries occurring in notes by *n*, and those for entries in tables by *t*.

Made in the USA
Monee, IL
04 November 2026

67379764R00085